HEAVEN'S ARSENAL
HELL'S DESTRUCTION

A Book On Spiritual Warfare

by LETICIA LEWIS

Foreword

"A City on a Hill Cannot Be Hidden , Neither do people light a lamp and hide it under a bowl."

In other words, if you have it, don't hide it, Let it shine! Our challenge is to remove the bowl of apathy, complacency, acquiescence and fear and once again lay claim to the stand of righteousness so that we may shine before all men.

We cannot be light until we embrace the following:

Today's complacency is tomorrow's captivity.

There is no such thing as comfortable Christianity.

You are what you tolerate!

Moral stagnation always leads to spiritual atrophy.

God did not give us a spirit of fear, but of power, love and sound mind.

What is trying to hide your light?

What is the name of the bowl?

We cannot deny that there exist a spiritual battle to turn off your light.

Forget Harry Potter and Hogwarts, via the conduit of biblical allusions, we know very well there are real spirits in the cities of the world today.

The Spirit of Pharaoh is alive holding people captive in the Egypt of spiritual and economic bondage and fear.

The spirit of Goliath still lives mocking and intimidating the children of God.

The Spirit of Jezebel still makes men and women hide in caves with sexual perversion and manipulation.

The Spirit of Absalom is dividing homes, churches and relationships while the Spirit of Herod is killing the young through violence, poverty, and sex trafficking murdering infant dreams and vision.

Yet I have news for you. There is a Spirit more powerful than all these spirits combined. Saints, we are here today to declare that the most powerful spirit alive today is not the spirit of Pharaoh, Saul, Absalom, Goliath, Jezebel or Herod, the most powerful Spirit on the Planet is the Holy Spirit of Almighty God, the Spirit of the Lamb.

"For it is not by might, nor by power, but by my Spirit saith the Lord", Zechariah 4:6.

For Where the Spirit of God is present there is freedom. 2 Corinthians 3:17

For where the Spirit of God is present there is power. Acts 1:8

So to every narrative and spirit that facilitates the platform of moral relativism, spiritual apathy, cultural decadence and ecclesiastical luke warmness we say the following: For every Pharaoh there must be a Moses, For every Goliath there must be a David, For every Nebuchadnezzar there must be a Daniel, for every Jezebel there must be an Elijah, for every Herod there must be a Jesus and for every devil that rises up against you there is a mightier God that rises up for you!

It is time to remove the bowl!

It is time to shake off whatever life or hell placed upon your light.

Rev. Dr. Samuel Rodriguez
President
NHCLC/CONELA
Hispanic Evangelical Association
Latinoevangelicals.com

Contents

Introduction:
Why Spiritual Warfare?

A s a child I grew up in church. I remember saying the "sinner's prayer" at age four, being baptized in water also at age four and at age eight I received the baptism of the Holy Spirit with the evidence of speaking in my heavenly prayer language, commonly referred to as speaking in Tongues. Speaking in tongues is a powerful spiritual weapon. Praying in our heavenly prayer language builds us up and brings revelation regarding any situation. I'm so grateful to the Lord for my mother who raised my siblings and me in the things of God. Although our dad did not attend church with us, we would pray for him while he stayed at home. My dad was not born again at the time.

I remember at the age of ten, I would go street witnessing with my brother, handing out tracts, and asking people if they knew Jesus as their Lord and personal Savior. I will never forget, when I handed a man a tract with a picture of a hearse on the front with the caption of 'are you going to church on your own or do you need help getting you there?' he was so startled after reading it, he handed the tract back to me.

It was in elementary school that I became acquainted with spiritual warfare. I even prayed binding and loosing satan and his demons in Jesus name. My mother would have my siblings and I pray often. We would get on our knees and pray to the Lord. Our prayers would include asking the Lord to bless our neighbors, protect us from all hurt, harm, and danger, and to heal people that were sick.

My childhood was both good and challenging. My dad was an excellent provider and we had want for nothing, yet there were days of verbal tirades and outbursts of anger. Even as a child, I knew this was nothing more than demonic influence. I knew this because of going to church, we were taught the Word of God and we were taught about some behaviors that can be demonically influenced.

My mother went to be with the Lord when I was only thirteen years old. It was because of my mother's love, and her love for the Lord that my siblings and I continued to serve the Lord, going to church, and as a result, I've been prepared by the Lord for such a time as this to release this book on Spiritual Warfare.

I remember when my sister and I were teenagers, we had just come home one evening, and our bedroom door was closed and the light in the kitchen was on. Surprisingly, there was a silhouette of a demon's face on the side of our bedroom door. We both looked at each other, looked at the silhouette, and I placed my hand over the shadow to see if it was the light in the kitchen reflecting off something in the house to project that image. That was not the case. My sister and I rose up with righteous spiritual indignation! We began to speak in tongues, plead the blood of Jesus, and say the name of Jesus, that image that shadow disappeared! We were so on fire and excited, knowing that the Lord is with us and that every demon must flee at the all powerful name of Jesus! Hallelujah!

Parents, your children need to learn to pray at an early age. They need to read their bible at an early age. They need to understand spiritual warfare at an early age. Even as the Lord is no respecter or persons, neither is the adversary. It is satan's desire to steal, and to kill, and to destroy (John 10:10) and he doesn't care about age. To God be the glory my dad is now born again, serving the Lord, and attending church on a regular basis. He always tells my sister and me that he loves us. My brother has also transitioned to Heaven at a young age, although I know he touched many lives for the Kingdom of God.

May you be blessed, encouraged, and equipped as you read this book. I will share with you the revelations the Lord has given to me based on the Word of God. This book on Spiritual Warfare will include military style strategies as given to me by the Holy Spirit.

> "To every *thing* there is a season, and a time to every purpose under the heaven: A time to get, and a time to lose; a time to keep, and a time to cast away; a time to rend, and a time to sew; a time to keep silence, and a time to speak; a time to love, and a time to hate; **a time of war, and a time of peace**."
>
> Ecclesiastes 3:1, 6-8 King James Version

Dedication:

I dedicate this book to my family; my parents Alton and Alexzine McCoy, to my siblings Reg and Michelle, and to my husband Don Lewis. My dad encouraged us in our dreams; my mother taught us prayer, and truly lived as a Proverbs 31 Woman. My siblings and I grew up as children truly hungered and thirst for the deeper things of God. My husband, Don is my constant support, advisor, and best friend.

Acknowledgments:

I would like to thank my Pastor, Dr. Samuel Rodriguez for allowing me to teach the Spiritual Warfare Class at our Spanish Church, Cantico Nuevo and at our English Church New Season Christian Worship Center for a year and a half! What a tremendous blessing!

I would also like to thank Pastor Phyllis Towles, one of the Associate Pastors for New Season Christian Worship Center for encouraging me to write this book!

Arsenal:

"A collection of weapons and military equipment
A place where weapons and military equipment are stored or made."

Oxforddictionaries.com

Destruction:

"The action or process of causing so much damage
to something that it no longer exists or cannot be repaired"

Oxforddictionaries.com

"Then he answered and spake unto me, saying This is the word of the Lord unto Zerubbabel, saying, Not by might, nor by power, but by my spirit, saith the Lord of hosts."

Zechariah 4:6 King James Version

Throughout scriptures, those who have accepted Christ Jesus as their Lord and Savior are referred to as Christians, Saints, Believers, and the Body of Christ. These words will also be used interchangeably throughout this book. The adversary who is satan, his name is deliberately in lower case. He tried to raise himself high, but he has been brought low by our Lord God Almighty!

Preface

⬧⬥⬧⬥⬧

Every born-again Christian without exception is engaged in Spiritual Warfare. The Word of God teaches us, "For though we walk in the flesh, we do not war after the flesh: **(for the weapons of our warfare are not carnal, but mighty through God to the pulling down of strong holds;)** Casting down imaginations, and every high thing that exalts itself against the knowledge of God, and bringing into captivity every thought to the obedience of Christ;" 2 Corinthians 10:3-5 King James Version. The New International Version reads, "For though we live in the world, we do not wage war as the world does. The weapons we fight with are not the weapons of the world. On the contrary, they have divine power to demolish strongholds. We demolish arguments and every pretension that sets itself up against the knowledge of God, and we take captive every thought to make it obedient to Christ."

The Message Translation reads, "The world is unprincipled. It's dog-eat-dog out there! The world doesn't fight fair. But we don't live or fight our battles that way—never have and never will. The tools of our trade aren't for marketing or manipulation, but they are for demolishing that entire massively corrupt culture. We use our powerful God-tools for smashing warped philosophies, tearing down barriers erected against the truth of God, fitting every loose thought and emotion and impulse into the structure of life shaped by Christ. Our tools are ready at hand for clearing the ground of every obstruction and building lives of obedience into maturity." These scriptures are clear in explaining that no Christian is exempt from Spiritual Warfare.

There are songs in some churches where the Saints would sing about being soldiers in the army of the Lord. This is very true. As previously stated, I will reference military style strategies in this book. The truth is every person who accepts Jesus as Lord and Savior is automatically drafted into the Service-God's service, His army. According to thefreedictionary.com, draft is defined as, "compulsory enrollment in the armed forces; conscription." Currently our military here in the United States of America is compromised of service men and service women on a voluntary basis and are not drafted into the armed forces.

As Christians, the draft is still enforced spiritually, yet we have the Good News which is we win! Our Lord has already given to us the victory over our adversary satan and all of his demonic entities. We must learn what are our Spiritual Weapons, and how do we use them?

Although we are in a spiritual battle, there is a time for war; however there is a time for peace.

What is spiritual warfare?

I've asked the Lord for the answer to this question and this is what He spoke to my spirit, "Spiritual warfare is unexplained oppositions in the natural realm because of demonic attacks that occur in the spirit realm." If you have ever asked yourself the question, "what is going on" that is usually a true indication of spiritual warfare.

Remember this, Christianity is not cotton candy. "Lest Satan should get an advantage of us: for we are not ignorant of his devices," 2 Corinthians 2:11 King James Version. There are demonic forces sent by satan to oppose every area of the lives of Believers. BUT, Glory be to God for we are more than conquerors through the Lord who loves us! "But no matter what comes, we will always taste victory through Him who loved us," Romans 8:37 the Voice translation. "No, despite all these things, overwhelming victory is ours through Christ, who loved us," New Living Translation. "But despite all this, **overwhelming victory is ours through Christ**

who loved us enough to die for us," the Living Bible Translation. (Bold added for emphasis). Our victory is ONLY in the Lord. We cannot defeat the adversary in and of ourselves, we need the Lord. Our Lord has already equipped His Church, the Body of Christ with spiritual weapons to overcome the forces of darkness! Glory to God!

Some of the information you will read, will sound radical. It's not radical but rather equipping you for spiritual warfare. We have spiritual weapons, now it is time to learn what they are and how to make full use of each and every one of them. Heaven's arsenal is surely hell's destruction!

I want to preface this book with this vital information; everything is NOT necessarily spiritual warfare. There are times in the lives of Believers that the pruning process is experienced (John 15:1-8). Pruning is a painful process as it is a cutting away of dead things or non-fruitful things. This can include but is not limited to the Lord allowing people to be removed, jobs or careers to be removed, family members to be removed, and attitudes and behaviors being corrected by the Lord to reflect Him. Anything that is not beneficial for His purpose and plans for your life can be "cut away."

Also, there are times when Believers are tried by fire. "And I will bring the third part through the fire, and will refine them as silver is refined, and will try them as gold is tried: they shall call on my name, and I will hear them: I will say, It is my people: and they shall say, The LORD is my God," Zechariah 13:9 King James Version. "Behold, I will send my messenger, and he shall prepare the way before me: and the LORD, whom ye seek, shall suddenly come to his temple, even the messenger of the covenant, whom ye delight in: behold, he shall come, saith the LORD of hosts. But who may abide the day of his coming? and who shall stand when he appeareth? for he is like a refiner's fire, and like fullers' soap: And he shall sit as a refiner and purifier of silver: and he shall purify the sons of Levi, and purge them as gold and silver, that they may offer unto the LORD an offering in righteousness," Malachi 3:1-3 King James Version.

This is necessary in the lives of Christians to trust the Lord in the midst of the "dross" or impurities being removed in order to become vessels of honor. "If you stay away from sin you will be like one of these dishes made of purest gold—the very best in the house—so that Christ himself can use you for his highest purposes," 2 Timothy 2:21 the Living Bible.

This is not a time of abandonment from the Lord, but rather purifying from unrighteousness to righteousness, from unholy to holy, and conforming to the image and likeness of the Lord. Therefore, I want to reiterate, refined by the fire of the Lord and being pruned by the Lord is not Spiritual Warfare. These are times of character building. In other words, if you are running late to church and you are in a vehicle by yourself on a Sunday morning and there is traffic, and you decide to break the law and enter into the carpool lane and the Highway Patrol pulls you over and gives you a ticket, that is not the time to rebuke the devil and say you are under attack with spiritual warfare. NO! You broke the law.

The Spiritual Warfare that will be explained in this book is in regards to demonic attacks of opposition that can appear in many forms; on the job, in relationships, where you live, and even going to church. Yes, going to church! This is referred to as "friendly fire" which is a military term. This will be discussed in more detail later in this book. Now, prepare your heart to receive revelation about your spiritual weapons and how to use them against the adversary, satan.

"My people are destroyed because they don't know me, and it is all your fault, you priests, for you yourselves refuse to know me; therefore, I refuse to recognize you as my priests. Since you have forgotten my laws, I will 'forget' to bless your children." Hosea 4:6 Living Bible

"My people are destroyed for lack of knowledge: because thou hast rejected knowledge, I will also reject thee, that thou shalt be no priest to me: seeing thou hast forgotten the law of thy God, I will also forget thy children." Hosea 4:6 King James Version

A lack of knowledge of the Word of God is what satan uses to bring destruction in the lives of people. As you read this book, you will gain wisdom, knowledge, and understanding regarding the revelation on Spiritual Warfare. You will not be destroyed for a lack of knowledge.

The Lord called me into the ministry and gave me the assignment of a prophetess. It is my responsibility to share the Word of God and the revelation or the rhema of His Word as given by the Holy Spirit. "GOD's Message came to me: "Son of man, speak to your people. Tell them, 'If I bring war on this land and the people take one of their citizens and make him their watchman, and if the watchman sees war coming and blows the trumpet, warning the people, then if anyone hears the sound of the trumpet and ignores it and war comes and takes him off, it's his own fault. He heard the alarm, he ignored it—it's his own fault. If he had listened, he would have saved his life. But if the watchman sees war coming and doesn't blow the trumpet, warning the people, and war comes and takes anyone off, I'll hold the watchman responsible for the bloodshed of any unwarned sinner. Ezekiel 33:3-6 the Message Translation.

The Voice Translation reads, "and if the lookout sees an army advancing toward the land and blows a trumpet to warn the people, and if someone hears the alarm and ignores it, allowing that army to come and capture him; then it is his own fault *for not taking appropriate action*. His blood will be on his own hands. If he had done something, he could have saved his life *and the lives of others*. But if the lookout sees an army advancing and does not sound the alarm to warn the people and if some are *captured or* killed, then their blood will be on the hands of the lookout."

The King James Version reads, "If when he seeth the sword come upon the land, he blow the trumpet, and warn the people; then whosoever heareth the sound of the trumpet, and taketh not warning; if the sword come, and take him away, his blood shall be upon his own head. He heard the sound of the trumpet, and took not warning; his blood shall be upon him. But he that taketh warning shall deliver his soul. But if the watchman see the sword come, and blow not the trumpet, and the people be not warned; if the sword come, and take any person from among them, he is taken away in his iniquity; but his blood will I require at the watchman's hand."

These scriptures cause reverential fear. It is my responsibility as a prophetess and the responsibility of all of those in Five Fold ministry to speak the truth in love and to warn the people of God of ensuing danger. If not, the Lord will require the blood of those on our hands who perish spiritually for not receiving the warning from the Lord. WHOA! Therefore because I know I will stand before the throne of the Lord one day and give an account I choose as a watchman on the wall to sound the alarm so no one's blood will be on my hands. Once the warning has come the outcome is no longer my account-ability or responsibility. This will be discussed in further detail when I expound upon psychics and mediums and others who are involved in witchcraft. This is diabolical. There is a call for repentance and if no repentance, eternal damnation and judgment.

> "For it is written, As I live, saith the Lord, every knee shall bow to me, and every tongue shall confess to God. So then every one of us shall give account of himself to God," Romans 14:11-12 King James Version.

> "For we must all appear before the judgment seat of Christ; that every one may receive the things done in his body, according to that he hath done, whether it be good or bad," 2 Corinthians 5:10 King James Version.

Part One:

Natural & Spiritual Soldiers

Chapter One:

The Department of Defense (Natural & Spiritual Military)

ere in the United States of America, we have the greatest military in the world. We have **five** military branches in which our
servicemen and servicewomen protect us from foreign and domestic
enemies. Our military include Air Force, Army, Marines, Navy, and
Coast Guard. Each branch is assigned to a specific area. Our military also have Special Operations Forces such as Air Force Special
Tactics, Army Green Berets, Marine Reconnaissance, and Navy Seals.
The Lord has called men and women into ministry and assigned them
to what is commonly referred to as the **Five**-Fold ministry gifts, or
ascension gifts; who are Apostles, Prophets, Evangelists, Pastors, and
Teachers, (Ephesians 4:11) for the purpose of "for the perfecting of
the saints, for the work of the ministry, for the edifying of the body of
Christ: Till we all come in the unity of the faith, and of the knowledge
of the Son of God, unto a perfect man, unto the measure of the stature
of the fullness of Christ:" (Ephesians 4:12-13 King James Version).

Do you see the parallel? Five branches for the armed forces
and five-fold for the Kingdom of God. This is not coincidence. The
United States of America was founded upon Christian principles
and ideals. "In God we trust." Even as the military have specific
assignments to protect and defend people in the natural, so do the

Five-Fold ministers have specific assignments from the Lord to also protect and defend people in the spiritual. "And there are diversities of **operations**, but it is the same God which works all in all," (1 Corinthians 12:6).

The nine gifts of the Holy Spirit in 1 Corinthians 12:8-10 are the special operations (special ops) of the power of God through the Holy Spirit. The United States military also have special operations, however under the same jurisdiction of the Department of Defense. Specialized training and operations for each branch are required. Even as special training in the Gifts of the Spirit are required.

The military have specific areas they are assigned to. As an example, according to Military.com, "the Air Force is the youngest of all five services. It became a separate service on Sept. 18, 1947 after President Harry S. Truman signed the National Security Act of 1947. In its more than 65 years of existence, the Air Force has become the world's premier aerospace force. Its mission simply put is to defend the nation through the control and exploitation of air and space. Although obviously tasked with flying missions, most personnel work on the ground in various construction, support, and technical capacities." According to Soldier.net, "the Air Force was created to defend the United States in the air as well as in outer space." The Air Force is advanced with top secret capabilities to carry out the mission. "The mission of the United States Air Force is to fly, fight and win ... in air, space and cyberspace," according to airforce.com.

As Christians, we have angels who are assigned to protect us spiritually; in the air, on the land, and in the sea. This will be expounded upon further after laying out the details of our great military, the armed forces. The Army is assigned to land and air. "The Strongest Force In The World. The U.S. Army is made up of the most dedicated, most respected Soldiers in the world. These Soldiers protect America's freedoms while serving at home and abroad, and they are always prepared to defend the nation in times of need. A U.S. Army Soldier is the embodiment of physical strength, mental strength and strength of purpose. As a Soldier, you will be prepared to serve our country whenever and wherever you are needed. You will be combat ready at all times, and you will be trained to counter any threat, any-where," goarmy.com. (bold added for emphasis).

The Marines are, "first to fight because of their culture and because they maintain a forward-deployed presence near various global hotspots," according to marines.com and as a result their commitment and training is "to defend our nation-in the air, on land, and at sea."

"The mission of the Navy is to maintain, train and equip combat-ready Naval forces capable of winning wars, deterring aggression and maintaining freedom of the seas" Navy Mission Statement, navy.com.

The United States Coast Guard (U.S. Department of Homeland Security) "For over two centuries the U.S. Coast Guard has safe-guarded our Nation's maritime interests in the heartland, in the ports, at sea, and around the globe. We protect the maritime economy and the environment, we defend our maritime borders, and we save those in peril. This history has forged our character and purpose as America's Maritime Guardian — *Always Ready* for all hazards and all threats. Today's U.S. Coast Guard, with nearly 42,000 men and women on active duty, is a unique force that carries out an array of civil and military responsibilities touching almost every facet of the U.S. maritime environment. The Coast Guard's motto is *Semper Paratus*, meaning "Always Ready," www.uscg.mil.

The United States of America is a humanitarian nation. This great Nation through our trained armed forces is always on alert to defend and protect our Nation's constitution, citizens and our allies. Interestingly enough, according to the United States Census Bureau, there are over three hundred and eighteen million people living in the U.S. and over seven billion people globally. That's a lot of people! The reality is the combined total of our armed forces is **less than** two million active duty men and women. **Therefore, there are less than two million people who are protecting literally hundreds of million people.** "There is no greater love than to lay down one's life for one's friends," John 15:13 New Living Translation.

Our military is compromised of men and women who lay down their lives for us on a daily basis. This is why Memorial Day and

Veteran's Day are so important for us to remember our soldiers' acts of valor and courage. We have a responsibility as Christians to pray for those who are enlisted in our armed forces from the Privates, to the Generals, to our Commander-In-Chief. We are forever grateful for the Department of Defense and for all of our Veterans; past, present, and future.

The Marines are the smallest in number yet the first to be deployed as the frontline fighters. In the military, it's the few protecting the masses. The Marine Corps motto "Semper Fidelis; Always Faithful. The Few. The Proud. The Marines." (www.Marines.com) So it is in the Kingdom of God. Scripture teaches us it is the Lord who chose twelve disciples and from those twelve men the Kingdom of God and the power of God was introduced to humanity starting in Jerusalem and Christianity spreading globally.

Even as there are a few men and women who serve in the military in relation to millions of civilians, there are only some chosen by the Lord for the equipping of the Church. Ephesians 4:11, "and he gave Some, apostles; and Some, prophets; and Some, evangelists; and Some, pastors and teachers," (capitalization added for emphasis). There are millions of Christians worldwide, however there are only some called into the specific assignment of the five fold ministry. Yet, all Christians, whether in ministry or not, are all called into the Army of the Lord. One of the names of the Lord used often in the Old Testament is the Lord of Hosts. This is a military name. It is also translated as Jehovah Sabaoth or the Lord of the Angel Armies. Christ Jesus is the Greatest military leader ever. He is the King of Kings and the Lord of Lords (Revelation 20:16).

Each military branch understands its assignment. The Navy understands protecting the seas, the Air Force understands protecting the air, and the Army understands protecting the land. They function according to what they are assigned to do and are trained efficiently to carry out each mission with success. It is imperative for the Body of Christ to understand the purpose and function of those called into the Five-Fold ministry as an assignment from the Lord. The Body of Christ is not comprised of Pastors only. The Pastors feed the Lord's flock for the local church. "And I will give you pastors according to mine heart, which shall feed you with knowledge and understanding," Jeremiah 3:15. Every born-again Christian needs to have a Pastor, no exceptions. "Not forsaking *or* neglecting to assemble together [as believers], as is the habit of some people, but admonishing (warning, urging, and encouraging) one another, and all the more faithfully as you see the day approaching," Hebrews 10:25 Amplified Version.

There is spiritual protection when Christians not just attend a local church, but rather join a local church and are submitted to the leadership the Lord established. It is the Lord who gives revelation in the Word of God and He anoints the pastor by the Holy Spirit to bring forth the rhema Word of God. "Every Scripture is God-breathed (given by His inspiration) and profitable for instruction, for reproof *and* conviction of sin, for correction of error *and* discipline in obedience, [and] for training in righteousness (in holy living, in conformity to God's will in thought, purpose, and action)," 2 Timothy 3:16 Amplified version. No, it is not enough to watch Christian programs on Television or attend Christian conferences, only. These should never take the place of having and being submitted to a Pastor.

Active duty military personnel are trained to understand the importance of submission and obedience to follow orders. They are also aware there are repercussions for not following orders. This training occurs in boot camp. So it is for Christians attending church on Sundays and at a mid-week Bible study. That is also boot camp because what is learned in church must be applied to day-to-day living. "Have confidence in your leaders and submit to their authority, because they keep watch over you as those who must give an account. Do this so that their work will be a joy, not a burden, for that would be of no benefit to you," Hebrews 13:13 New International Version.

> "Obey your spiritual leaders and submit to them [continually recognizing their authority over you], for they are constantly keeping watch over your souls *and* guarding your spiritual welfare, as men who will have to render an account [of their trust]. [Do your part to] let them do this with gladness and not with

sighing *and* groaning, for that would not be profitable
to you [either]," Hebrews 13:17 Amplified Version.

"Listen to your leaders and submit to their authority
over the community, for they are on constant watch
to protect your souls and someday they must give
account. Give them reason to be joyful and not to
regret their duty, for that will be of no good to you,"
Hebrews 13:17 Voice Translation.

I had a prophetic prayer line for three consecutive years. Every
Saturday morning I would be on the prayer line, praying for people
and prophesying into their lives as the Holy Spirit gave me what
to say. One of the questions I consistently asked each caller was,
"are you a member of a local church?" Surprisingly, many gave
the same answer which was an astounding no. There are so many
"un-churched" Believers who seem to wander spiritually with no
guidance and no spiritual covering. This is not the will of the Lord.
There were Apostles who joined me on the prayer line as well. It
was truly awesome to see the Lord touch the lives of His people and
minister to them through yielded vessels bringing forth, wisdom,
knowledge, and understanding, clarity, rebuke, and encouragement.
"For the Lord gives wisdom; from his mouth come knowledge and
understanding," Proverbs 2:6 New International Version. "Preach the
word; be prepared in season and out of season; correct, rebuke and
encourage—with great patience and careful instruction," 2 Timothy
4:2 New International Version.

The Lord spoke to my heart or to my spirit one day and said,
"Those who church hop and do not join a local church and become
a member and submit to the authority I have chosen over my House
are spiritually AWOL." WHOA! Spiritually AWOL Lord?! Yes, spiritually AWOL. Ok that's deep. That blew me away. Why? Because
AWOL is a military acronym for "absent without leave" or "absent
without official leave." Spiritual leaders have the God-given responsibility to watch over the souls of the Lord's people. I'm not talking
about people who try to spiritually manipulate, dominate, or control,

I'm talking about those called by the Lord with specific instructions according to the Word of God to watch and protect the Lord's people. Therefore, those Christians who leave a church for whatever reason and wander from church to church are absent from their spiritual duties and therefore have no spiritual covering for protection.

The Five Fold ministry is called and chosen by the Lord to function in the Body of Christ. It is dangerous for a pastor to not allow, Apostles, Prophets, Evangelists or Teachers to speak and declare and decree what thus sayeth the Lord. When a pastor rejects another ministry gift, then that Pastor is rejecting God. It is the Lord who chooses, calls, and anoints not man. People must understand that the five fold ministry offices are not glorified man made titles, but rather God-given callings. I've heard people say, 'well I am not into titles.' This is a person who needs to be taught the importance of honor. "That's why whenever we can we should always be kind to everyone, and especially to our Christian brothers," Galatians 6:10 the Living Bible Translation. I've also heard men say of a Pastor, 'he's not better than me. He puts his pants on one leg at a time just like I do.' Again, that's not the point. The military understands honor. A private cannot disrespect a general without repercussions. It's called order and authority. So it is for the Body of Christ to understand the Kingdom of God and His way of establishing spiritual order and authority. We all have an adversary and yielding to the Lord's ways will tend to a life of power, victory, and manifestations of provisions and blessings.

Chapter Two:

Military Assignments

A very profound passage of scripture in the words of our Lord, "You have not chosen me, but I have chosen you, and ordained you, that you should go and bring forth fruit, and that your fruit should remain: that whatsoever you shall ask of the Father in my name, he may give it you," John 15:16 King James Version. This is what our servicemen and servicewomen understand. Their superiors are chosen as high ranking officials for a specific task in the military and for them to carry out their duties and specific orders as assigned. Christians need to stop looking at those in ministry as just another person, but rather understand they are called by God, not called in and of themselves and to understand with that calling comes great responsibility. "For unto whomsoever much is given, of him shall be much required," Luke 12:48b King James Version. Recognize the calling of God on someone's life according to the Word of God. Spiritual authority is established by the Lord.

Even as each of the five branches of the military have specific areas they're assigned to; land, sea, and air, they also use different tactical weapons and artillery based on those locations. M180, hand grenades, missiles, rocket launchers, Mark 50 torpedo, machine guns, etc. are specific weaponry for specific branches. In addition to these weapons and others that are highly classified, each branch also have Special Operations or Special Operations Forces. These are highly trained, and a highly sophisticated team to carry out special classified missions. Even the Five Fold ministry gifts have specific operations in the gifts of the Spirit, (1 Corinthians 12:8-10).

Again, as all Christians are called into the Army of the Lord. There are also other gifts assigned to the Body of Christ by the Holy Spirit, "and God has set some in the church, first apostles, secondarily prophets, thirdly teachers, after that miracles, then gifts of healings, helps, governments, diversities of tongues," 1 Corinthians 12:28 King James Version. Although you might not be called into the Five Fold ministry per se, that does not mean you are not gifted by the Lord in other areas such as miracles, helps, or governments. Everyone in the military is not trained for Special Operations yet every assigned duty for every soldier is important.

"So we, *being* many, are one body in Christ, and individually members of one another. Having then gifts differing according to the grace that is given to us, *let us use them:* if prophecy, *let us prophesy* in proportion to our faith; or ministry, *let us use it* in *our* ministering; he who teaches, in teaching; he who exhorts, in exhortation; he who gives, with liberality; he who leads, with diligence; he who shows mercy, with cheerfulness," Romans 12:5-8 New King James Version. Each person in the Body of Christ have different gifts, yet we are one Body. The military have different branches, yet are all under the Department of Defense.

There are those who have the gift of prophecy, yet that does not mean they are called into the office of a prophet. That gift is still important and necessary. There are those with the gift of mercy or the gift of giving. These gifts do not necessarily equate to full time ministry, yet they are important and necessary to be a blessing to others. Those in the military who are not trained in Special Ops are not jealous of nor try to hinder those who are trained in Special Ops. Therefore, the Body of Christ needs to stop showing jealousy, envy or even try to hinder those who are called by the Lord into the Five Fold Ministry and operate in the gifts of the Spirit.

The various components of our Department of Defense are highly classified in regards to missions and training, however each branch has elite trained soldiers for Special Operations or Special Forces.

The United States Army have Army Rangers, Delta Force, and Green Berets, the United States Air Force have Air Commandos, the United States Marine Corps have Reconnaissance, the United States Navy have the Seals, and the United States Coast Guard have (DOG), Deployable Operations Group. This is not necessarily a fully exhaustive description of the Specials Ops for each military branch; however this is information available to the general public, especially for those considering a career in the military. The rigorous training for each Special Operation or Special Operations Force is more extensive than the general boot camp training. Each soldier must endure this training in order to be fit for the military. Therefore, all soldiers do not have the same training or mission assignments.

This is also true with us as "military" Christians. As Christians, we are all one Body, yet we have separate functions. "For just as each of us has one body with many members, and these members do not all have the same function, so in Christ we, though many, form one body, and each member belongs to all the others," Romans 12:4-5 New International Version. Also, "just as a body, though one, has many parts, but all its many parts form one body, so it is with Christ," 1 Corinthians 12:12 New International Version. These passages of scriptures will be expounded upon in more depth later.

In addition to our Department of Defense, there is the NSA (National Security Agency), who works to support military operations. The NSA in summary is a Government agency established for the purpose of network warfare. This is the information from their website: "The majority of our nation's intelligence for counterterrorism, hard targets and support to military operations comes from the National Security Agency /Central Security Service. For the good of the nation, it is imperative that NSA/CSS maintain its cryptologic superiority." GEN Keith Alexander–Director NSA/Chief CSS. "The National Security Agency/Central Security Service (NSA/CSS) is home to America's codemakers and codebreakers. The National Security Agency has provided timely information to U.S. decision makers and military leaders for more than half a century. The Central Security Service was established in 1972 to promote a full partnership between NSA and the cryptologic elements of the armed forces.

NSA/CSS is unique among the U.S. defense agencies because of our government-wide responsibilities. NSA/CSS provides products and services to the Department of Defense, the Intelligence Community, government agencies, industry partners, and select allies and coalition partners. In addition, we deliver critical strategic and tactical information to war planners and war fighters.

By its very nature, what NSA/CSS does as a key member of the Intelligence Community requires a high degree of confidentiality. Our Information Assurance mission confronts the formidable challenge of preventing foreign adversaries from gaining access to sensitive or classified national security information. Our Signals Intelligence mission collects, processes, and disseminates intelligence information from foreign signals for intelligence and counterintelligence purposes and to support military operations. This Agency also enables Network Warfare operations to defeat terrorists and their organizations at home and abroad, consistent with U.S. laws and the protection of privacy and civil liberties. NSA/CSS exists to protect the Nation. The Information Assurance mission confronts the formidable challenge of preventing foreign adversaries from gaining access to sensitive or classified national security information. The Signals Intelligence mission collects, processes, and disseminates intelligence information from foreign signals for intelligence and counterintelligence purposes and to support military operations. This Agency also enables Network Warfare operations to defeat terrorists and their organizations at home and abroad, consistent with U.S. laws and the protection of privacy and civil liberties," www.nsa.gov. In summary, the NSA have the capabilities to monitor phone calls, emails, and other forms of communication whether through computer systems or telephone systems.

In essence, with the advancement of technology, wars and war strategies have also advanced to protect this Nation and our allies. Warfare has now advanced to technological strategies. "But Daniel, keep this prophecy a secret; seal it up so that it will not be understood until the end times, when travel and education shall be vastly increased!" (Daniel 12:4 the Living Bible).

Although there are major wars, i.e. World War 1, World War 2, Korean War, Vietnam War, Gulf War, War in Afghanistan, our servicemen and servicewomen are prepared for deployment at anytime for the mission at hand. Our military Special Ops are trained to go into other countries to gather "Intel" or Intelligence. Even as we sleep peacefully every night, our military are literally on missions around the world to protect us and our allies. Again, let us continue to pray for our military and for their protection.

I highly recommend everyone to watch the movie "Zero Dark Thirty." After the attack on American soil which occurred on Tuesday, September 11, 2001 often referred to as 9/Eleven, because of the date, (911 the emergency distress call for help), war had taken on new strategy in warfare. Over 3,000 lives were lost, and although there have been countless documented stories of miracles and heroism, the greatest man hunt of all time took eminent precedence. "Zero Dark Thirty" is a movie based on the true story of the Special Operations elite team the Navy Seals, who had the assignment of locating and eliminating the world's most dangerous man, Osama bin Laden. There was actual news footage that was later released showing the Commander-in-Chief, "President Obama watch the mission unfold at the White House along with Vice President Joe Biden, Defense Secretary Robert Gates, and Secretary of State Hillary Clinton, alongside other Security staff, including Chairman of the Joint Chiefs Admiral Mike Mullen, National Security Adviser Tom Donilon, and Counter-Terrorism chief John Brennan," http://www.dailymail.co.uk/news/article-1382859/Osama-bin-Laden-dead-Photo-Obama-watching-Al-Qaeda-leader-die-live-TV.html.

The Lord Jesus spoke these words, "You will hear of wars and rumors of wars, but see to it that you are not alarmed. Such things must happen, but the end is still to come," Matthew 24:6 New International Version.

The previous military information provided will be connected as a parallel with natural wars and spiritual wars as it pertains to military branches and spiritual callings into the ministry by the Lord.

Chapter Three:

Nine Spiritual Weapons

—◁◁◁◁◁∫ʃ▷▷▷▷—

"For the weapons of our warfare are not carnal, but mighty through God to the pulling down of strong holds,"   2 Corinthians 10:4 King James Version.

I would read the above scripture over the years and ask myself, 'what are our spiritual weapons?' Our weapons plural, more than one, are what we have as Christians to live mighty victorious lives over the plots, plans, and schemes of the adversary. I finally asked the Lord one day in prayer and He gave me nine spiritual weapons that we need to use in our spiritual warfare. I'm not saying there are only nine, there could be more; however the Lord gave me nine that I will show you in scripture. These spiritual weapons are not categorized according to importance, they are all equally important and one does not have more precedence over the other, except for the all powerful Name of Jesus.

Weapon Number One: the Word of God.

The Word of God is priority for the lives of Believers. Unfortunately too many Christians use their Bibles as a part of the furniture on the coffee table in the Living Room area of their home. The Bible, the Word of God is Jesus in written form. "Then said I, Lo, I come: in the volume of the book it is written of me," Psalm 40:7 King James Version and "then I said, "Look, I have come. As is written about me in the Scriptures," Psalm 40:7 New Living Translation.

The scriptures are often referred to as Logos, which is a Greek word according to Strong's Exhaustive Concordance defined as a word, the Word. Notice when Word is capitalized. The capitalization is indicative of referring to the Lord. "In the beginning was the Word, and the Word was with God, and the Word was God," John 1:1 King James Version. The Word of God is our powerful weapon against the adversary and all of the forces of darkness! Satan is a liar and the father of lies (John 8:44). Whenever we speak forth as a confession of faith or to declare and decree the Word of God, it causes change and will also refute and overcome the lies of the adversary. Hallelujah! When the Lord fasted for forty days and nights in the wilderness, satan came with his temptations. The Lord conquered the adversary in every area of life making redemption and victory for all mankind through salvation in His blood. Glory!

What Adam and Eve did not do in the Garden of Eden, the Lord accomplished and conquered in the wilderness. The first Adam failed, the last Adam succeeded with eternal victory (1 Corinthians 15:45). The Lord stepped out of divinity and wrapped Himself in humanity (1 Corinthians 15:47). When the devil spoke with temptations the Lord said, "IT IS WRITTEN," (Luke 4:1-13 capitalization added for emphasis). The Word of God is the most powerful book in the universe and the devil knows it, that's why he distracts Christians from spending time reading their Bible. Satan went to Eve in the Garden of Eden in the form of a serpent and twisted the instructions from the Lord regarding the food they were to eat and deceiving her (Genesis 3:1-5). The devil also tempted Jesus with food. He didn't stop there. He tempted the Lord and used scripture to quote to Him. He quoted Psalm 91:11-12. That is amazing. The archenemy came to the Lord quoting the Word of God! The Lord responded once again with the Word of God, quoting Deuteronomy 6:16. Therefore, satan was able to quote that scripture because he was once the anointed cherub (Ezekiel 28:14). This will be discussed in further detail in later chapters.

Many Christians ask the question, "How do I know the voice of the Lord? How do I know when it is the Lord speaking to me?" In order to know His voice is to know His Word. The Bible is not a novel, a self help book, a handbook, or some periodical. The Bible is medicine to the sick, healing to the infirmed, joy to the joyless, and love to the loveless, hope to the hopeless, faith to the faithless. It is a well of life, and it is Christ Jesus! Questions you might have are found in the Word of God. No person has all the answers. Only the Lord is all powerful, all knowing, and all wise. He is everywhere at the same time, Omnipresent. He is all powerful, Omnipotent. He is all knowing and all wise Omniscient. That is why He is the Alpha and the Omega, the First and the Last, (Revelation 1:8, 11, 17 and Revelation 22:13). Any problems in life that you might face, the answers are in the Word of God. Study your Bible. Read it. Meditate on it. Memorize it. Declare and decree the Word of the Lord over every area of your life. The Lord said we as His sheep know His voice and we will flee from the voice of strangers (John 10:4-5, 14, 16, and 27).

Weapon Number Two: Praise and Worship

All throughout scriptures, we read where mighty miracles ensued as a result of praising and worshipping the Lord prior to a battle and after the battle was fought and won. "But thou art holy, O thou that inhabits the praises of Israel," Psalm 22:3. The Hebrew word, Yashab teaches us that when the Lord inhabits our praise, He is abiding, dwelling, remaining, and sitting in the place of our praise! That is powerful! The Lord is so worthy to receive all of our praise and for us to worship Him in spirit and in truth (John 4:24).

Weapon Number Three: Fasting

Eating can create an atmosphere of camaraderie and hospitality. However, when it comes to needing breakthroughs from the Lord, and pulling down strong holds, it is a necessity to turn down the plate. I often say, if a person abstains from food, and does not pray or read their Bible that is nothing more than a glorified diet. Fasting causes the spiritual senses as it were to become more keen and alert. Hearing the voice of the Lord can become even clearer. Receiving in depth instructions from Him, becoming sensitive to the leading of the Holy Spirit, as well as an increase in the anointing are powerful results of fasting. There is nothing wrong with prayer breakfasts, and ministry luncheons, yet when there is a time of fasting and seeking the Lord, there is supernatural power that is released. The Lord even said to His disciples when He cast out a demon spirit from a man, this kind goes out by prayer and fasting, (Matthew 17:21 & Mark 9:29).

Weapon Number Four: Tithes and Offerings

Malachi 3:7-12 King James Version
7 Even from the days of your fathers ye are gone away from mine ordinances, and have not kept them. Return unto me, and I will return unto you, saith the LORD of hosts. But ye said, Wherein shall we return? 8 Will a man rob God? Yet ye have robbed me. But ye say, Wherein have we robbed thee? In tithes and offerings.
9 Ye are cursed with a curse: for ye have robbed me, even this whole nation.
10 Bring ye all the tithes into the storehouse, that there may be meat in mine house, and prove me now herewith, saith the LORD of hosts, if I will not open you the windows of heaven, and pour you out a blessing, that there shall not be room enough to receive it.
11 And I will rebuke the devourer for your sakes, and he shall not destroy the fruits of your ground; neither shall your vine cast her fruit before the time in the field, saith the LORD of hosts.
12 And all nations shall call you blessed: for ye shall be a delightsome land, saith the LORD of hosts. (**Lord of hosts bolded for emphasis**).

For years I have read these passages of scripture and what always stood out to me was that the Lord of hosts is referenced four times in these particular scriptures. I knew in my spirit, this was one of many names for the Lord but what does it mean exactly? Why is the Lord of Hosts identified repeatedly? Who is the Lord referencing Himself as? There are many names of God to help us relate to His many attributes.

Well, it was on a Wednesday night while at Bible Study at my church New Season Christian Worship Center when I received the revelation. My Pastor, Dr. Samuel Rodriguez was preaching the Word on a totally different subject yet he referenced the Lord of Hosts. He said it is translated Jehovah Sabaoth meaning the Lord of the Angel Armies. It was at that moment my spirit received the rhema or the revelation of the Word of God regarding this scripture. The Lord later in my prayer time began to expound upon this and what this means in which He is identifying Himself in a military term that He is the One over the Angel Armies leading the charge against the devil and his demons. Glory to God! It's not Michael the warring Archangel leading the charge but rather the Lord Christ Jesus Himself as the Lord of the Angel Armies! Militarily, the Lord personally gets involved in rebuking the devourer on our behalf when we give Him what is His. The ten percent tithe and the offerings are His.

Weapon Number Five: Prayer

There are many types of prayer. For the sake of Spiritual Warfare, I will only cover eight. There is the prayer of; Binding and Loosing (Matthew 16:19, Matthew 18:18), Agreement (Matthew 18:19-20), Intercession (Genesis 18:22-33, Ezekiel 22:30,) -Tongues/Heavenly Prayer Language (Acts 1:8, Acts 2:4), Supplication (Philippians 4:6), Faith (James 5:15), Dedication and Consecration (Luke 22:42 and James 4:7), Thanksgiving (multiple chapters in Psalm).

Weapon Number Six: Forgiveness

The Lord shared with me in my time of prayer, that forgiveness is not the lack of accountability, but rather forgiveness allows the Lord access to avenge the one who experienced wrong doing. Oftentimes, when a person thinks of forgiving someone, it is almost as if the recipient of forgiveness is getting away with doing wrong. That is not true. Romans 12:19 reads, "Dearly beloved, avenge not yourselves, but rather give place unto wrath: for it is written, **Vengeance is mine; I will repay, saith the Lord,**" (King James Version bold added for emphasis). The Lord does not want His children to go around getting revenge or being vindictive towards others. He does not want His children to have a vendetta towards anyone. Also, it is imperative to forgive others in order to receive forgiveness from the Lord. The Lord said in Mark 11:25-26, "And when you stand praying, forgive, if ye have ought against any: that your Father also which is in heaven may forgive you your trespasses. But if you do not forgive, neither will your Father which is in heaven forgive your trespasses," King James Version. Therefore it is important to note that prayer and forgiveness coincide. In times of prayer forgive others, and the Heavenly Father will forgive you. Do not forgive, and one cannot expect to be forgiven from the Father. Giving and receiving forgiveness is an action that gives the Lord access for Him to avenge of wrongdoing. And the Lord's vengeance always far exceeds any act one can do on his own.

Weapon Number Seven: the Name of Jesus

The name of Jesus is above every other name, whether in heavenly realms or in earthly realms. The demons tremble in fear at His name. Every knee will bow to His name. Bodies are healed, the dead are raised, and circumstances change because of His name. The all powerful name of Jesus! It is imperative for Christians to pray and close out their prayers in the name of Jesus. Praying and closing the prayer by saying amen only is likened unto a person who receives a check in a large sum of money. The funds are available to deposit or cash the check, however if there is no signature on the check, the check is null and void.

"Wherefore God also has highly exalted him, and given him a name which is above every name: That at the name of Jesus every knee should bow, of things in heaven, and things in earth, and things under the earth; And that every tongue should confess that Jesus Christ is Lord, to the glory of God the Father," Philippians 2:9-11. Salvation is only in the all powerful name of Jesus. "And it shall come to pass, that whosoever shall call on the name of the Lord shall be saved," Acts 2:21 King James Version and "for whosoever shall call upon the name of the Lord shall be saved," Romans 10:13. And Acts 4:12 clearly states "neither is there salvation in any other: for there is none other name under heaven given among men, whereby we must be saved."

It is only in the name of Jesus for salvation, in the name of Jesus to command demons to flee, in the name of Jesus for victory in every area of life. The name of Jesus is all powerful. When we pray, we say in Jesus name and then amen which means so be it.

Weapon Number Eight: the Blood of Jesus

The Blood of Jesus, washes away sins, heals, protects, and delivers. I remember growing up in church as a little girl and singing songs about the Blood. These songs were a part of the worship service and were not sung only on Communion Sunday. Oh we would sing about the Blood. The Blood that Jesus shed for me. Sadly, there are people who bled to death due to wounds that could not be treated in a timely manner. Oh but the Blood of Jesus! Our Lord should have bled to death because of the brutal thirty-nine stripes or beatings He received. But He could not bleed to death because His blood had to be shed for all mankind. The Lord emphasized the importance of communion, "Then Jesus said unto them, Verily, verily, I say unto you, Except you eat the flesh of the Son of man, and drink his blood, you have no life in you. Whoso eats my flesh, and drinks my blood, has eternal life; and I will raise him up at the last day. For my flesh is meat indeed, and my blood is drink indeed. He that eats my flesh, and drinks my blood, dwells in me, and I in him. As the living Father has sent me, and I live by the Father: so he that eats me, even he shall live by me. This is that bread which came down from heaven: not as your fathers did eat manna, and are dead: he that eats of this bread shall live forever," John 6:53-58.

We have victory because of the Blood of the Lamb! "And they overcame him by the blood of the Lamb, and by the word of their testimony; and they loved not their lives unto the death," Revelation 12:11. When the Children of Israel were about to make their mass Exodus from Egypt, they received specific instructions from the Lord. "Then Moses called for all the elders of Israel, and said unto them, Draw out and take you a lamb according to your families, and kill the passover. And ye shall take a bunch of hyssop, and dip it in the blood that is in the bason, and strike the lintel and the two side posts with the blood that is in the bason; and none of you shall go out at the door of his house until the morning. For the LORD will pass through to smite the Egyptians; and when he sees the blood upon the lintel, and on the two side posts, the LORD will pass over the door, and will not suffer the destroyer to come in unto your houses to smite you," Exodus 12:21-23.

If the Lord did not allow the destroyer to hurt anyone when He saw the blood of an animal on the exterior of their houses, how much more when we plead the Blood of Jesus are we protected from hurt, harm and danger? The Blood of Jesus is powerful!

Weapon Number Nine: Love

God is love! It is interesting that many Christians are challenged to say "I love you." There are those who can say "love you" with a response from the other party of "love you too!" or "love ya." And then there's the classic cliché' of "I love you with the love of the Lord." Why is it so difficult for people to say the words, "I love you?" Could it be perhaps, because society has equated love with romance only? In the Greek language there are four separate words used to describe love; Agape, Éros, Philia, and Storgē.

Agape love is commonly referred to as the highest form of love. This is unconditional love. This love is expressed from the Lord to all mankind and from His Sons and Daughters expressed to Him. Éros is referred to as sensual or passionate love. Philia is referred to as love expressed between friends, relatives, and even community. Storgē is referred to as love expressed between parents and their child or children.

Love is a weapon because faith works by love, Galatians 5:6. Without faith it is impossible to please God, Hebrews 11:6. In order to properly use any of the spiritual weapons in our heavenly arsenal provided by the Lord, they must be accessed and utilized by faith. However, if a person is not walking in love, could it be possible their faith is weak or perhaps defunct? Apart of our Armor of God, Ephesians 6:13-17, the Shield of Faith is what we use to quench ALL of the fiery darts of the wicked. Could it be possible that fiery darts from the wicked are penetrating the Shield of Faith if the person's love walk is not strong?

Considering there are four different types of love, then which love does faith work by? In the Greek dictionary of the New Testament, love is translated from the original word Agape, defined as affection or benevolence, charity. It is important to continue to abide in a place of agape love, the Lord's love; the highest form of unconditional love because in doing so, the Lord is properly represented.

Eros love is found in the book of the Songs of Solomon. This love is a beautiful expression of intimacy and passion between a man and his wife with intimacy and tenderness. This love needs to be intact between married couples as prayers can be hindered if the husband does not honor his wife, 1 Peter 3:7.

Philia, or philadelphos in 1 Peter 3:8, is defined as fond of brethren, love as brethren, or brotherly love. This is why the city of Philadelphia in the state of Pennsylvania is known as the "City of Brotherly Love."

Storgē is the love between parents and children. According to the Word of God, parents who do not correct or discipline their children do not love them. "He who spares his rod hates his son, but he who loves him disciplines him promptly," Proverbs 13:24 New King James Version.

Chapter Four:

Combat Ready

N one of these spiritual weapons will work without Believers being totally committed and submitted to the Lord. In this era of receiving revelation about the blessings of the Lord, we must remain totally dependent upon the Lord. It seems as though there are some Christians who place more faith in having faith and using their faith, rather than having a consistent deep relationship and fellowship with the Lord. We must keep our faith in the Lord rather than having faith in the faith given to us by the Lord. After all, we receive our faith from God, Romans 12:3.

The Lord said "I am the vine, and you are the branches. If you abide in Me and I in you, you will bear great fruit. Without Me, you will accomplish nothing," John 15:5 the Voice translation. The emphasis here is that without the Lord we will accomplish **nothing!** We must stay connected to the Lord and not go astray. Engaging in the inevitable of spiritual warfare which is the life for all Believers, means remaining totally dependent upon the Lord.

In the military, there are repercussions for privates who do not follow the instructions of their superiors. The same holds true for us as Believers. We must obey the Lord to avoid the repercussions of disobedience.

Chapter Five:

Spiritual Enemy Entities

―⸻⸎⸻―

T he reality is there are only two types of people in the earth popu-
lated by literally billions of people. Saved and unsaved. That's it,
no in between. Therefore, every day we encounter people who know
the Lord as their Lord and Savior, and people who have satan as their
father. This is why we must put on the WHOLE armor of God. The
armor of God is protection against unseen diabolical forces sent to
oppose us. "Finally, my brethren, be strong in the Lord, and in the
power of his might," Ephesians 6:10. Here in this passage of scripture, we are exhorted or urged to be strong, not in self, not in one's
own abilities or intellect, but rather to be strong in the Lord and in
the power of his might. The word power in this scripture is translated from the Greek word kratos which means dominion. Therefore
as Believers, we are to be strong in the Lord and in His dominion,
might, power, and strength.

Every Christian has been given dominion and power from the
Lord over the adversary satan and his demonic hierarchy. Satan's
hierarchy consists of principalities, powers, rulers of the darkness of
this world, spiritual wickedness in high places, Ephesians 6:12. The
opposition and attacks we encounter is not with people per se, but
derive from these evil spirits who use people. The word principalities
is the Greek word arche which is defined as magistrate or rule and a
magistrate is an officer of the state or a judge.

In essence, evil principalities are evil spirits that have their jurisdiction in the court system. This is why it is evident that there is much corruption in the judicial system. There are criminals who have been found guilty yet do not serve time for their crimes due to "technicalities." Innocent people have lost their lives through death row sentencing also referred to as capital punishment only for it to be discovered later their innocence was in fact correct. But unfortunately their bodies decay and rot in a grave that was not meant for them to be buried in.

Although there is the Due Process of Law which is supposed to be "a fundamental, constitutional guarantee that all legal proceedings will be fair and that one will be given notice of the proceedings and an opportunity to be heard before the government acts to take away one's life, liberty, or property. Also, a constitutional guarantee that a law shall not be unreasonable," thefreedictionary.com. However, in the world system which is not governed by Christians there are times it appears as though it is the "injustice" system. At times the one with the most money to hire the best attorney wins. These evil spirits influence Government. This nation is experiencing the aftermath of prayer being taken out of schools. Laws are passed that are in opposition to the Word of God and such laws that violate our First Amendment right. This Amendment is supposed to protect the citizens' rights for religious freedom. Christianity in America is under much persecution and that Amendment which was established by the Forefathers of this nation which was once irreprehensible, now the notion of legislators subpoenaing the notes of Christian clergy is now at hand.

Powers in the Greek is the word exousia, defined as delegated influence, authority, jurisdiction, strength. Powers are evil spirits that come to attack people individually. These demons desire to take control over a person's mind, and they can possess people who are sinners and try to oppress Believers with depression also referred to in the Bible as a spirit of heaviness. Demons have jurisdiction over certain territories. This is why you can travel on the same street for miles at a time and watch the neighborhood change from poverty to prosperity or vice versa. The mentality of a home-owner can have a noticeable difference from a person who rents a home. Why is that? This is because of the mentality of value or lack thereof.

Powers come to influence or have jurisdiction over the thoughts of people's lives. Examples of their evil activity include pornography, drugs, both legal and illegal, alcohol, music, and even movies and Television programs. This is why as Christians we cannot use clichés such as "praise the Lord like you've lost your mind." NO! We have the mind of Christ, Philippians 2:5. Mental illness is on the rise. Satan does not care about cute clichés or slang terms.

Even as the angels of the Lord respond to our words when we speak the Word, so do demonic spirits respond to our words when we speak certain words. Drugs, alcohol, and pornography are all attributed to having mind altering affects. Powers are behind such. I remember when my husband and I were out shopping. We decided to shop at a store that is Christian owned. As we walked in, the instrumental music of "How Great Thou Art" was playing over the speakers. I noticed the shoppers were pleasant and the store was very peaceful. After we completed our shopping, we went to another national retail store close by. There was secular music playing over the speakers and the mood of the shoppers was vastly different. People were rude, children were running around, and the shopping experience was somewhat disheartening in comparison to what we experienced moments earlier. Music can have an effect on the mind and the mind effects mood.

Some Christians believe it is okay to drink wine for health benefits or to drink alcohol on occasion to unwind and relax. Our bodies are the temple of the Holy Spirit, 1 Corinthians 6:19. When alcohol is consumed, that person becomes under the influence. After all, isn't it interesting that alcohol is referred to as wine AND spirits? The consumption of alcohol; beer, wine, or some other form of an intoxicating beverage can cause a person to act in a way that is not his or her true personality. The person's speech can change and their thinking and judgment can become impaired. A good way to relax or unwind is to take a hot bubble bath, drink herbal tea, and take vitamins and minerals. This will help the physical body and not subtly ail the physical body.

The Greek word for pharmacy is Pharmakeia, which is the practice and making of medication and vitamins. Interestingly, it also refers to "the making of spell-giving potions or elixirs believed to have transforming powers, such as the ability to extend life, boost energy, or enhance the mind." In the Bible, the word is translated as "witchcraft" or "sorcery." Isn't it interesting that the modern word for pharmacy is translated as witchcraft in the Bible? (Referenced by Wikipedia). This is another example of powers. Even with all of the drug commercials advertising products that can help treat certain illnesses always comes with the warning of the side effects. Some of the side effects that are mentioned include nightmares, inability to sleep, hallucinations, thoughts of suicide, and even depression.

Spiritual wickedness in high places are demonic spirits that influence false religions. Cults, false prophets, false apostles, and false religions are a result of these evil spirits. This is indicative of the Word of God which teaches us that satan himself is transformed into an angel of light, (II Corinthians 11:14). This is the epitome of deception. Remember, satan is the antichrist. He is the one who opposes all things Christian.

Rulers of the darkness of this world are demons that influence fortune-telling, palm reading, familiar spirits, mediums, white and black magic, psychics, witches, warlocks, Ouija boards, etc. Christians are not to participate in any of these nor are they to read "horror scopes" as I call it. Again, satan's deception is through intrigue. As the Lord spoke to my heart one day, He said "Deception is a thin slice of truth wrapped around a lie." The rulers of the darkness of this world have the appearance of sounding true. Talking to the dead is nothing more than a demon in disguise. Horoscopes sound true based on birthdays and months. Remember this, satan and all of the fallen angels are evil wicked spirits. They were around before man was ever created. Therefore the wicked one has observed the behaviors and patterns of mankind since the beginning of time.

This is why it is imperative for every church to allow the Holy Spirit to operate as He chooses to. His Gifts, the gifts of the Spirit are for people to be edified, encouraged, warned, and receive confirmation and direction for their lives. People know there is more to life and often wonder what is the real road map to acquire success? When the prophets speak by the Holy Spirit, He is the one who is leading and guiding people in truth and not leading people astray.

Part Two:

Lock and Load

Chapter Six:

Armed for Deployment

━━⊶⊷━━

L ock and load is a military term which means "be ready and prepared." We see this as an admonition in scripture, "be sober, be
vigilant; because your adversary the devil, as a roaring lion, walks
about, seeking whom he may devour," 1 Peter 5:8. This scripture
teaches us that satan is on the prowl and if he is seeking to devour,
that means he cannot devour everyone. It is not the Lord's will for our
Spiritual Weapons to be dormant, underutilized, or not fully engaged.

It is imperative for Christians to not only know what are our spiritual weapons, but also to understand how to use each of the nine
spiritual weapons in our heavenly arsenal against the forces of darkness. Now that you know you have spiritual weapons, now it is time
to learn how to use them.

Spiritual Weapon #1 the Word of God

As we read in Genesis chapter one, "and God said" is repeated
several times in scripture. Every time we read these passages, "God
said," is God the Son speaking; Jesus Christ who is the Word. "In
the beginning was the Word, and the Word was with God, and the
Word was God. The same was in the beginning with God. All things
were made by him; and without him was not anything made that was
made," John 1:1-3.

Sadly, too many Christians attend a weekly church service and seldom open their Bibles and read scripture. This is dangerous. When satan came to tempt Jesus in the wilderness, the Lord overcame every temptation by speaking the Word, by saying it is written. Satan is still the tempter. He will always be a deceitful wicked tempter, however how will Christians know how to overcome his vices, if they do not know the Word of God? Oh yes, we can have conferences, seminars, symposiums, etcetera, however how many Christians are walking away equipped in the Word of God?

"Then was Jesus led up of the Spirit into the wilderness to be tempted of the devil. And when he had fasted forty days and forty nights, he was afterward an hungered. And when the tempter came to him, he said, If thou be the Son of God, command that these stones be made bread. But he answered and said, It is written, Man shall not live by bread alone, but by every word that proceeds out of the mouth of God.

Then the devil takes him up into the holy city, and sets him on a pinnacle of the temple, And said unto him, If thou be the Son of God, cast thyself down: for it is written, He shall give his angels charge concerning thee: and in their hands they shall bear thee up, lest at any time thou dash thy foot against a stone. Jesus said unto him, It is written again, Thou shalt not tempt the Lord thy God. Again, the devil takes him up into an exceeding high mountain, and shows him all the kingdoms of the world, and the glory of them; And said unto him, All these things will I give thee, if you wilt fall down and worship me. Then said Jesus unto him, Get thee hence, Satan: for it is written, Thou will worship the Lord thy God, and him only will you serve. Then the devil leaves him, and, behold, angels came and ministered unto him," Matthew 4:1-11. Now in the book of Luke, the scripture reads, "and when the devil had ended all the temptation, he departed from him for a SEASON," Luke 4:13 (capitalization added). Now if the devil came to tempt Jesus, why do so many Christians act as though his evil temptations have ceased? Interestingly in Luke, the scripture teaches that the devil left the Lord for a season. A season is only for a certain period of time. Therefore, the devil certainly came back tempting the Lord again. This is why many Christians in America need to repent for not reading their Bible. There are Christians in other countries around the world who are literally being killed for reading their Bible. Here in the United States too many treat the Word of God as a part of the furniture in their living room, having "the Good Book" opened yet not reading or studying scripture. Remember, the Lord said His people are destroyed for a lack of knowledge, (Hosea 4:6).

There are 66 books in the Bible, 39 in the Old Testament and 27 in the New Testament. Yes, there's a lot of controversy about lost scrolls and books that might have been removed from the original compilation of scripture. I frequently suggest do something with the 66 books you do have rather than be concerned about the ones you don't have.

Ephesians 6:10-17 is very clear we are to be strong in the Lord and in the power of His might and for us to put on the WHOLE armor of God. The armor is for protection. We have a weapon included with our armor which is the Sword of the Spirit, the Word of God.

Finally, my brethren, be strong in the Lord, and in the power of his might.

> [11] Put on the whole armour of God, that ye may be able to stand against the wiles of the devil.
> [12] For we wrestle not against flesh and blood, but against principalities, against powers, against the rulers of the darkness of this world, against spiritual wickedness in high places.
> [13] Wherefore take unto you the whole armour of God, that ye may be able to withstand in the evil day, and having done all, to stand.
> [14] Stand therefore, having your loins girt about with truth, and having on the breastplate of righteousness;
> [15] And your feet shod with the preparation of the gospel of peace;
> [16] Above all, taking the shield of faith, wherewith ye shall be able to quench all the fiery darts of the wicked.

[17] And take the helmet of salvation, and the sword of
the Spirit, which is the word of God

(King James Version)

Verse seventeen admonishes take the Sword of the Spirit which is the Word of God. The Word is a sword in the realm of the spirit. Hebrews 4:12, "for the word of God is quick, and powerful, and sharper than any two edged sword, piercing even to the dividing asunder of soul and spirit, and of the joints and marrow, and is a discerner of the thoughts and intents of the heart. "For whatever God says to us is full of living power: it is sharper than the sharpest dagger, cutting swift and deep into our innermost thoughts and desires with all their parts, exposing us for what we really are," The Living Bible translation.

The Word of God not only causes us to resist the devil and he will flee as we are submitted to God, (James 4:7), the Word also changes us so we can become conformed to the image and likeness of God. We cannot expect Christians to live holy just by telling them to do so. It is imperative to spend time reading the Bible, meditating on scriptures, memorizing scriptures, and decreeing and declaring the Word of God. "I beseech you therefore, brethren, by the mercies of God, that ye present your bodies a living sacrifice, holy, acceptable unto God, which is your reasonable service. And be not conformed to this world: but be ye transformed by the renewing of your mind, that ye may prove what is that good, and acceptable, and perfect, will of God," Romans 12:1-2. The Word of God teaches us to "study to shew yourself approved unto God, a workman that needs not to be ashamed, rightly dividing the word of truth," 2 Timothy 2:15.

This is the reason it is imperative for all Five of the ministry offices to be in operation, Apostles, Prophets, Evangelists, Pastors and Teachers (Ephesians 4:11). One of the functions for Apostles and Prophets is to bring correction to doctrinal error, i.e. using scripture out of context.

As previously stated when the devil came to tempt Jesus, even as the Lord responded to each temptation with the Word, the Lord was speaking of Himself. Jesus is the Word. The devil is aware of scripture as well. The devil had the audacity to tempt Jesus and then use scripture to try to justify his temptation!

"Then the devil takes him up into the holy city, and sets him on a pinnacle of the temple,

And said unto him, If you be the Son of God, cast thyself down: for it is written, He shall give his angels charge concerning you: and in their hands they shall bear you up, lest at any time you dash your foot against a stone.

Jesus said unto him, It is written again, You will not tempt the Lord your God," Matthew 4:5-7 King James Version.

Satan was literally quoting Psalm 91:11-12! "For he shall give his angels charge over thee, to keep thee in all thy ways. They shall bear thee up in their hands, lest thou dash thy foot against a stone."

This is why as Christians, it is imperative to not only read the Word of God but to also study the Word of God to know the difference between the traditions of men and logos or rhema Word of the Lord. "Making the word of God of no effect through your tradition which you have handed down. And many such things you do," Mark 7:13. This is why as Christians we need to ask questions, get clarity and not just arbitrarily accept teachings just because. This is why even throughout the pages of this book, I am not just referencing scriptures, I am also including the scriptures. It will behoove you to go back and reread the scriptures I've shared and not just accept it as truth because of a quote and reference. STUDY the Word of God for yourself.

In the military, the soldiers have night vision goggles. They can be in the most remote, darkest place on the planet, yet when they turn on those goggles everything around them is illuminated. The Lord spoke to my heart, "the same is true for my Word." And then He spoke to my heart the scripture, "Thy word is a lamp unto my feet, and a light unto my path," Psalm 119:105. That is powerful! The Word of God illuminates! We are the light of the world. Our Lord is the greatest light.

4 In him was life; and the life was the light of men.
5 And the light shineth in darkness; and the darkness comprehended it not.   (John 1:4-5)

The Word of God is like having spiritual night vision goggles. The light of the Lord is in us as Christians. We shine in darkness. We are light.

Now the Holy Spirit has given those in what is referred to as the Five Fold Ministry (Apostles, Prophets, Evangelists, Pastors and Teachers; Ephesians 4:11) revelation of the scriptures to help those who read the Word to understand and receive clarity of the Word.

"Now an angel of the Lord spoke to Philip, saying, "Arise and go toward the south along the road which goes down from Jerusalem to Gaza." This is desert. [27] So he arose and went. And behold, a man of Ethiopia, a eunuch of great authority under Candace the queen of the Ethiopians, who had charge of all her treasury, and had come to Jerusalem to worship, [28] was returning. And sitting in his chariot, he was reading Isaiah the prophet. [29] Then the Spirit said to Philip, "Go near and overtake this chariot."

[30] So Philip ran to him, and heard him reading the prophet Isaiah, and said, "Do you understand what you are reading?"
[31] And he said, "How can I, unless someone guides me?" And he asked Philip to come up and sit with him.
[32] The place in the Scripture which he read was this:
"He was led as a sheep to the slaughter;
And as a lamb before its shearer *is* silent,
So He opened not His mouth.
[33] In His humiliation His justice was taken away,
And who will declare His generation?
For His life is taken from the earth."
[34] So the eunuch answered Philip and said, "I ask you, of whom does the prophet say this, of himself or of some other man?"
[35] Then Philip opened his mouth, and beginning at this Scripture, preached Jesus to him.
[36] Now as they went down the road, they came to some water. And the eunuch said, "See, *here is* water. What hinders me from being baptized?"

³⁷Then Philip said, "If you believe with all your heart, you may." And he answered and said, "I believe that Jesus Christ is the Son of God."

³⁸ So he commanded the chariot to stand still. And both Philip and the eunuch went down into the water, and he baptized him. ³⁹ Now when they came up out of the water, the Spirit of the Lord caught Philip away, so that the eunuch saw him no more; and he went on his way rejoicing,"   Acts 8:26-39.

As scripture is clear here, a man of great authority was reading scripture or in that time the scrolls of the Prophet Isaiah. Although he was reading the Word, he did not have clarity of the Word. Philip was an Evangelist, (Acts 21:8) and was used mightily of the Lord. Philip was able to bring clarity to the man who read the Word, yet read with no understanding. The Lord gives those called into the Ministry understanding and revelation of the Word of God to help Christians grow in the knowledge of God.

We have an account of the power of the Sword of the Spirit which is the Word of God in the book of Revelation. "Now out of His mouth goes a sharp sword, that with it He should strike the nations. And He Himself will rule them with a rod of iron. He Himself treads the winepress of the fierceness and wrath of Almighty God," Revelation 19:15. I'm going to reference this scripture again later as I expound upon the Lord being the Lord of Hosts which is a military term. Christ Jesus is the Word and from His mouth goes a sharp sword. This is an indication of the power of God we have every time we open our mouths and speak the Word of God. It is a sharp sword!!

There are times Christians will quote Job, "though he slay me, yet will I trust in him: but I will maintain mine own ways before him," Job 13:15. First of all, Job was unaware of the conversation about him between the Lord and satan. He was saying that although the Lord is bringing me this calamity I will still maintain my ways of sacrificing to Him and serving Him. The Lord did not bring calamity to Job, nor was He slaying anyone. THE LORD WAS NOT DOING THIS TO JOB, IT WAS SATAN! In the Old Testament, the Jewish people were not aware of demonic spirits. There is not one scripture in the Old Covenant of anyone casting out a demon. Satan is the one who kills, steals and destroys. The Lord gave satan permission to do just that.

Job 1:6-12
>⁶Now there was a day when the sons of God came to present themselves before the LORD, and Satan came also among them.
>⁷And the LORD said unto Satan, Whence comest thou? Then Satan answered the LORD, and said, From going to and fro in the earth, and from walking up and down in it.
>⁸And the LORD said unto Satan, Hast thou considered my servant Job, that there is none like him in the earth, a perfect and an upright man, one that feareth God, and escheweth evil?
>⁹Then Satan answered the LORD, and said, Doth Job fear God for nought?
>¹⁰Hast not thou made an hedge about him, and about his house, and about all that he hath on every side? thou hast blessed the work of his hands, and his substance is increased in the land.
>¹¹But put forth thine hand now, and touch all that he hath, and he will curse thee to thy face.
>¹²And the LORD said unto Satan, **Behold, all that he hath is in thy power; only upon himself put not forth thine hand. So Satan went forth from the presence of the LORD.** (Bold added for emphasis).

In verse one; Job was described as being an upright man who hated evil. "There was a man in the land of Uz, whose name *was* Job; and that man was blameless and upright, and one who feared God and shunned evil," New King James Version. Job's own wife even told him to curse God and die.

⁹Then his wife said to him, "Do you still hold fast to your integrity? Curse God and die!"

¹⁰But he said to her, "You speak as one of the foolish women speaks. Shall we indeed accept good from God, and shall we not accept adversity?" In all this Job did not sin with his lips.

(Job 2:9-10 New King James Version).

Notice what the scripture reavealed-in all this Job did not SIN WITH HIS LIPS! This is why as Christians reading the Bible is of utmost importance. It is imperative! It will keep us from sinning with our lips, meaning our words. The Lord also said we are justified and we are condemned by our words. (Matthew 12:37 King James Version). "The words you say will either acquit you or condemn you," (Matthew 12:37 New Living Translation). This is why as Christians we cannot use our words loosely. In fact when we all stand before the Lord to give an account for the life we live, we will also be judged by our words spoken. The Lord said, "but I tell you, on the day of judgment men will have to give account for every idle (inoperative, nonworking) word they speak," (Matthew 12:36 Amplified Version of the Bible). This is why we can no longer quote Job trying to sound deep as if the Lord is slaying us when He's not. The Word of God convicts us, convinces us, transforms us, heals us, brings revelation regarding any situation, brings us peace, hope, love, joy, etc.

The Word is Jesus and the Word of God is a spiritual weapon against satan and his demonic forces. Now, this is what we are encouraged to do from the book of Job, "you shall also decide *and* decree a thing, and it shall be established for you; and the light [of God's favor] shall shine upon your ways," Job 22:28 Amplified Version. How will Christians know what to decide and decree if they're not spending time studying the Word of God? Too many Christians are giving satan access to their lives because of the words they speak. Remember this; there are two forces at work in this earth realm at all times; the Kingdom of God and the kingdom of darkness.

That's why Christians need to stop saying 'just praise the Lord like you're losing your mind.' NO! Mental illness is real. The angels of the Lord respond to our words or are spiritually deployed when we speak the Word of God. Demonic spirits respond to our words also when words of doubt and unbelief are spoken. So if you're unmarried, stop saying 'I can do badly all by myself' because that's exactly what will start happening. New Age uses terminology of putting your words out in the universe and let the universe bring back to you what you want. The devil is a liar! As what was stated earlier, the Word is Jesus, the Sword of the Spirit which is a part of our armor is the Word of God. No, this is not extreme. This is spiritual warfare and spiritual warfare is real.

Here are some examples of how to use your Sword:

Daily you should declare and decree these scriptures over your life. I'm only going to provide chapter and verse so you can look up the scriptures for yourself.

1. Genesis 12:3
2. Psalm 3:5
3. Psalm 91:1-16
4. Proverbs 10:7
5. Isaiah 53:4-5
6. Isaiah 54:17
7. Zechariah 4:6
8. Malachi 3:8-12
9. Luke 6:38
10. Romans 8:31 & 37
11. Philippians 4:13
12. Philippians 4:19
13. 1 Peter 2:24
14. 1 John 1:9
15. 1 John 4:4

The Lord is the ONLY King who will NEVER be dethroned! He has no term limits! He was, is, and always will be (Revelation 1:8.) He is the Alpha and the Omega. He is the beginning and the ending. In the United States of America, the President is the Commander In Chief as it pertains to the highest rank in the Country. This is the

President's title. There is a balance of power in this country. The President is subject to Congress, so it is spiritually. The Lord is the Greatest Power in the Universe and in the spirit realm. He is sovereign and He is the Highest rank. Yet, He is subject to His spiritual congress per se. The spiritual congress is His Word. "For you have magnified your Word above all your name," Psalm 138:2b. The Lord's Word is a powerful weapon against the forces of darkness! Every time we speak the Word of God, our Sword is going forth. The devil has to flee at the Word of God. Speak the Word not the circumstances. Put your angels to work for you. The angels are here to help you succeed in life and to protect you.

When Christians speak the Word of God, their angels are deployed. The angels understand the language of Heaven. My native language is English. If someone who speaks Italian attempted to have a conversation with me, we would not be able to communicate. Why? This is because their language is foreign to me. It is not native. So it is for the angels of God. When we speak words of doubt and unbelief, we are speaking a foreign language. That is not the language of Heaven. The angels cannot respond to the foreign language of doubt and unbelief. They only understand the language of the Word of God.

Spiritual Weapon #2 Praise and Worship

There are many scriptures in the Bible that teach us the power of our praise and worship. The book of Psalms is a book of a compilation of songs and praises. When we praise and worship the Lord, mighty things happen on our behalf. Too many Christians receive answers to their prayers and seldom thank the Lord. The Lord is not pleased with murmuring or complaining. Doing so, is sinning with our lips as stated earlier which is what Job did not do. If you've found yourself murmuring or complaining, stop right now and repent to the Lord, asking Him for forgiveness and then go into praise and worship.

When the children of Israel were brought out of Egypt, Miriam sang and danced before the Lord.

²⁰ Then Miriam the prophetess, the sister of Aaron, took a timbrel in her hand, and all the women went out after her with timbrels and dancing.

²¹ And Miriam responded to them, Sing to the Lord, for He has triumphed gloriously *and* is highly exalted; the horse and his rider He has thrown into the sea.

(Exodus 15:20-21 Amplified Version).

The Lord's presence abides in our praises!

³ But thou art holy, O thou that inhabitest the praises of Israel, (Psalm 22:3).The word inhabitest in Hebrew means yashab, which means to sit down, to dwell, to remain. This is so powerful! Every time we praise and worship the Lord, His presence comes in and His Spirit sits down in our midst, dwells with us and remains! Glory to God! That is why praise and worship is so important in a church service. People can get healed from all types of sickness and disease, and infirmities and ailments because where the presence of the Lord is, demonic spirits are driven out! Hallelujah! This is why praise and worship should not be timed or limited to a program as a part of going through a religious motion. Instead, it is a time when corporately the people of God begin to praise and worship, and shout and rejoice and dance before the Lord. Yes even dance before the Lord! David danced before the Lord, Miriam the prophetess and other ladies with her danced before the Lord, and we are admonished to dance before the Lord!

³ **Let them praise his name in the dance**: let them sing praises unto him with the timbrel and harp,

(Psalm 149:3).

Our Lord is great and He is greatly to be praised. When we sing, dance, and worship the Lord, ambushes are set up against the forces of darkness.

> [22] And when they began to sing and to praise, the LORD set ambushments against the children of Ammon, Moab, and mount Seir, which were come against Judah; and they were smitten.
> [23] For the children of Ammon and Moab stood up against the inhabitants of mount Seir, utterly to slay and destroy them: and when they had made an end of the inhabitants of Seir, every one helped to destroy another.
> [24] And when Judah came toward the watch tower in the wilderness, they looked unto the multitude, and, behold, they were dead bodies fallen to the earth, and none escaped.
> [25] And when Jehoshaphat and his people came to take away the spoil of them, they found among them in abundance both riches with the dead bodies, and precious jewels, which they stripped off for themselves, more than they could carry away: and they were three days in gathering of the spoil, it was so much,
> (2 Chronicles 20:22-25). Read the entire chapter for the full context.

Here in scriptures, the enemies of the children of Israel turned on each other and killed each other. AND the children of Israel carried away the spoils of war which took them THREE days to gather everything it was so much. Too many Christians experience spiritual warfare yet do not walk away with the spoils of war. They have nothing to show for their victory. In the New Testament we know that our war is not with flesh and blood but against principalities, against powers, against the rulers of darkness of this world, against spiritual wickedness in high places, (Ephesians 6:12).

This is why all music is not Gospel music. Oftentimes when the word Gospel music is utilized, it usually denotes a certain genre. But Gospel means "good news," therefore whenever a singer of gospel songs, or a choir, quartet, etc. sings songs, the purpose is to usher the presence of the Lord so ambushments can be set up against demonic spirits, glory to God. That's why singers of gospel music should not sing songs of fatigue, defeat, or weariness. The presence of the Lord does not inhabit that. After all, the Word of God teaches us let the weak say I am strong, (Joel 3:10b).

Our songs should be songs of victory and adoration and love for the Lord and His glorious might and strength. Our praise, worship, and dance before the Lord are mighty spiritual weapons. This is why when gospel artists charge a certain amount of money in order to come "minister" at someone's church or conference, what if that church is not functioning at a certain budget? Does that mean then, the anointing that is to be on the music and on the artist cannot be shared with the rest of the Body of Christ which is supposed to usher in the presence of the Lord God Almighty, Him glorified? Well the Lord spoke on hirelings, but that's another book.

Satan knows how powerful praise and worship is, after all when he was Lucifer, the Bible says he was an anointed cherub.

Here is a description of Lucifer in scriptures.

> [12] Son of man, take up a lamentation upon the king of Tyrus, and say unto him, Thus saith the Lord GOD; Thou sealest up the sum, full of wisdom, and perfect in beauty.
> [13] Thou hast been in Eden the garden of God; every precious stone was thy covering, the sardius, topaz, and the diamond, the beryl, the onyx, and the jasper, the sapphire, the emerald, and the carbuncle, and gold: the workmanship of thy tabrets and of thy pipes was prepared in thee in the day that thou wast created.
> [14] Thou art the anointed cherub that covereth; and I have set thee so: thou wast upon the holy mountain

of God; thou hast walked up and down in the midst of the stones of fire.

¹⁵ Thou wast perfect in thy ways from the day that thou wast created, till iniquity was found in thee.

¹⁶ By the multitude of thy merchandise they have filled the midst of thee with violence, and thou hast sinned: therefore I will cast thee as profane out of the mountain of God: and I will destroy thee, O covering cherub, from the midst of the stones of fire.

¹⁷ Thine heart was lifted up because of thy beauty, thou hast corrupted thy wisdom by reason of thy brightness: I will cast thee to the ground, I will lay thee before kings, that they may behold thee.

¹⁸ Thou hast defiled thy sanctuaries by the multitude of thine iniquities, by the iniquity of thy traffick; therefore will I bring forth a fire from the midst of thee, it shall devour thee, and I will bring thee to ashes upon the earth in the sight of all them that behold thee.

¹⁹ All they that know thee among the people shall be astonished at thee: thou shalt be a terror, and never shalt thou be any more,   (Ezekiel 28:12-19).

These verses teach us that Lucifer was perfect and beautiful, until iniquity was found in him.

¹² How art thou fallen from heaven, O Lucifer, son of the morning! how art thou cut down to the ground, which didst weaken the nations!

¹³ For thou hast said in thine heart, I will ascend into heaven, I will exalt my throne above the stars of God: I will sit also upon the mount of the congregation, in the sides of the north:

¹⁴ I will ascend above the heights of the clouds; I will be like the most High.

¹⁵ Yet thou shalt be brought down to hell, to the sides of the pit.

16 They that see thee shall narrowly look upon thee, and consider thee, saying, Is this the man that made the earth to tremble, that did shake kingdoms;
17 That made the world as a wilderness, and destroyed the cities thereof; that opened not the house of his prisoners?
18 All the kings of the nations, even all of them, lie in glory, every one in his own house.
19 But thou art cast out of thy grave like an abominable branch, and as the raiment of those that are slain, thrust through with a sword, that go down to the stones of the pit; as a carcass trodden under feet.
20 Thou shalt not be joined with them in burial, because thou hast destroyed thy land, and slain thy people: the seed of evildoers shall never be renowned,

(Isaiah 14:12-21).

Satan is very much aware of the power of praise and worship and how the Godhead is moved, stirred, and blessed by such praises and such worship. This is the reason why the music industry is heavily influenced by demonic activities because even now satan still looks to be worshipped. This was even one of the temptations he presented to the Lord. Satan actually wanted the Lord to bow down to him (Matthew 4:9). This is the reason I can boldly say with confidence that I can give you a guarantee that just about every church has challenges, problems, isms, schisms, jealousy, and envy in their choirs or with their praise team or worship leaders. There are those who get mad if they can't sing lead, or can't direct the choir. Some even end up leaving the church, the place where the Lord sent them. Why is this? The devil knows the power of praise and worship and he hates it. When we praise and worship the Lord, the Lord is still setting up ambushments, but it's on the works of darkness. When we praise and worship the Lord, we are inviting Him to abide in and dwell in our presence. When we praise and worship the Lord demons turn on each other and fight each other.

^{6} Let the high praises of God be in their mouth, and a two-edged sword in their hand;
^{7} To execute vengeance upon the heathen, and punishments upon the people;
^{8} To bind their kings with chains, and their nobles with fetters of iron;
^{9} To execute upon them the judgment written: this honour have all his saints. Praise ye the LORD

(Psalm 149:6-9).

These scriptures are indicative of spiritual warfare against demonic entities. When we praise the Lord with our mouths and lift our hands before Him in praise, worship, and adoration, our hands become as a two-edged sword. The binding of kings and nobles are not in the literal sense of people, but rather that's what happens to demonic forces. There is a real life account of the power of praise when a child was kidnapped from in front of his home.

"On the night of March 31, (2015), 9-year-old Willie Myrick was playing with his pet chihuahua outside his Atlanta home when a man grabbed him and forced him into a car, police said.

"He was cursing at me telling me to shut up and didn't want to hear a word from me," Willie told ABC affiliate WSB-TV. "He said if I told anyone, he would hurt me, like in a bad way."

But according to a report this week by NBC affiliate WXIA-TV, not remaining silent may have saved Willie's life.

A lover of gospel music, Willie, who just turned 10 this week, reportedly started singing the song "Every Praise" until the man — who had been driving around for almost three hours — finally threw him onto the street and drove away.

"Every praise is to our God," the gospel song begins. "Every word of worship with one accord."

Touched by Willie's story, Hezekiah Walker, the songwriter behind "Every Praise," flew to Atlanta this week to meet the young man. Walker told WSB-TV that he believes God spoke through him to "save that boy's life."

"You never know who you're going to touch," the gospel singer said.

According to CBS Atlanta, there's $10,000 reward for the capture of the man who kidnapped Willie. The suspect is described as a black male in his mid- to late-20s. He is said to have been wearing khaki shorts and a white, short-sleeve shirt with a Nike logo at the time of the abduction," www.huffingtonpost.com.

This is the power of praise! Praise is a powerful spiritual weapon against satan and all of his demons.

"150 Praise ye the LORD. Praise God in his sanctuary: praise him in the firmament of his power.

> ²Praise him for his mighty acts: praise him according
> to his excellent greatness.
> ³Praise him with the sound of the trumpet: praise him
> with the psaltery and harp.
> ⁴Praise him with the timbrel **and dance:** praise him
> with stringed instruments and organs.
> ⁵Praise him upon the loud cymbals: praise him upon
> the high sounding cymbals.
> ⁶Let every thing that hath breath praise the LORD.
> Praise ye the LORD,"
>   (Psalm 150:1-6, bold added for emphasis).

This is why it's dangerous for Christians to deliberately be late to church and miss praise and worship so they can receive the Word only. Yet, during the week, they'll have secular music playing on the radio in their car or Sports Utility Vehicle, (SUV). Corporate praise and worship honors the greatness of our God and invites His presence into the church service.

This spiritual weapon is not only for Sundays and midweek Bible study. This is actually to be a lifestyle for Believers.

> ¹⁹Speaking to yourselves in psalms and hymns and
> spiritual songs, singing and making melody in your
> heart to the Lord;

[20] Giving thanks always for all things unto God and
the Father in the name of our Lord Jesus Christ;"
(Ephesians 5:19-20).

Let the word of Christ dwell in you richly in all wisdom; teaching
and admonishing one another in psalms and hymns and spiritual
songs, singing with grace in your hearts to the Lord, (Colossians
3:16). This scripture emphasizes the importance of the words of
Christ, which are the words of the Anointed One to dwell in us richly
in all wisdom. The words of Christ are the words in the Bible. With
modern technology, it is now possible to listen to praise and worship
music on the computer, on cell phones, and other electronic devices.
If there are a lot of disturbances in your home, if your children are
experiencing nightmares and bad dreams, play praise and worship
music in your home. Allow your children to go to sleep at night
with praise and worship music playing. They will wake up refreshed
and peaceful.

When the adversary comes with his attacks, use your spiritual
weapon of praise and worship against him and watch the atmosphere
in your home change. If your place of work is negative, and if you're
allowed to utilize the company computer to play personal Compact
Discs (CD's), or given permission to go to a website of a Christian
artist and play their music, do so. As long as you keep the music low
enough for you to hear, trust and believe the atmosphere of the presence of the Lord will change any environment. When we worship
the Lord, our angels worship with us. In fact the seraphim cry Holy,
Holy, Holy.

6 In the year that king Uzziah died I saw also the LORD sitting
upon a throne, high and lifted up, and his train filled the temple.

[2] Above it stood the seraphims: each one had six
wings; with twain he covered his face, and with twain
he covered his feet, and with twain he did fly.
[3] And one cried unto another, and said, Holy, holy,
holy, is the LORD of hosts: the whole earth is full of
his glory.

⁴And the posts of the door moved at the voice of him
that cried, and the house was filled with smoke,
(Isaiah 6:1-4).

The presence of the Lord is not limited to a church service or event. Worship, praise and dance before the Lord in your home and expect His presence, His glory, His power to show up. And where the presence of the Lord is, demonic activity must flee. Hallelujah!

Spiritual Weapon #3 Fasting

⁶Is not this the fast that I have chosen? to loose the
bands of wickedness, to undo the heavy burdens, and
to let the oppressed go free, and that ye break every
yoke?   (Isaiah 58:6).

"This is the kind of fast day I'm after: to break the
chains of injustice, get rid of exploitation in the work-
place, free the oppressed, cancel debts,"
(Isaiah 58:6 The Message Translation).

There is power in turning away from food, or turning down the plate as it were. The Lord tells us in His Word that bands of wickedness are loosed, heavy burdens are undone, those dealing with oppression will be set free, and that every yoke which is bondage will be broken. When you go on a fast, be prepared for people to come with unexpected "blessings" to take you out to lunch, for someone on the job to suggest a group luncheon, cookies delivered to you, etc. These are temptations for you to break your fast. Don't do it. Fasting causes the voice of the Lord to become even more clear, for clarity regarding different situations to come forth with greater understanding and revelation, and breakthroughs to occur.

One of the most powerful accounts of the power of corporate fasting is described in the book of Esther. The Jewish people were fearful of being killed.

> [13] And the letters were sent by posts into all the king's
> provinces, to destroy, to kill, and to cause to perish, all
> Jews, both young and old, little children and women,
> in one day, even upon the thirteenth day of the twelfth
> month, which is the month Adar, and to take the spoil
> of them for a prey, (Esther 3:13 King James Version).

Queen Esther was admonished by Mordecai, her family member that who knows whether she is come into the kingdom for such a time as this to save their lives (Esther 4:14). She heeded the warning and admonishment and this was her response:

[16] Go, gather together all the Jews that are present in Shushan, and fast ye for me, and neither eat nor drink three days, night or day: I also and my maidens will fast likewise; and so will I go in unto the king, which is not according to the law: and if I perish, I perish, (Esther 4:16).

The results were supernatural intervention. The Jewish people's lives were saved and their enemies were killed. When we do corporate fasting, people's lives are saved and demonic forces and strongholds are pulled down and demolished! Hallelujah!

There are different types of fasts. There's what is commonly referred to as the Daniel Fast. This is derived from Daniel 10:3 when the prophet fasted for 21 days.

> [3] I ate no pleasant bread, neither came flesh nor wine in
> my mouth, neither did I anoint myself at all, till three
> whole weeks were fulfilled,   (King James Version).

There is also a juice only or liquid fast, where only 100% pure juice and water are consumed. And there is the Esther Fast. This is a total abstinence fast. Some people including myself have gone for three consecutive days with no food and no water as a time of fasting and really seeking the Lord, praying and reading scriptures.

If you are under a doctor's care for health or medical issues, consult with your physician prior to any fasts. The Daniel Fast is a healthy fast for those who are on medication. There is a proper way of starting a fast and breaking a fast. It is recommended that you prepare your body for the change in consumption and digestion by gradually coming off meat, bread, sweets, coffee, soda, etc. And once your fast is broken, you want to gradually eat solid foods again but it's best to start with broth and fruits and vegetables.

As I always say, if a person is abstaining from food, yet not spending time reading the Bible and praying, that is nothing more than a glorified diet. Fasting is a spiritual experience which yields many great benefits. If you're married, it's best to get permission from your spouse prior to starting a fast.

> [5] Do not deprive one another except with consent for a time, that you may give yourselves to fasting and prayer; and come together again so that Satan does not tempt you because of your lack of self-control,
> (1 Corinthians 7:5 New King James Version).

If there is a strong hold in your life, such as drinking, smoking, using illegal drugs, addicted to prescription drugs, using profanity, viewing pornography, wrath, jealousy, etc. anything that you cannot overcome on your own and receiving wise counsel has helped but has not delivered you, or if you know of someone experiencing these bondages and strongholds, fasting will bring forth deliverance! People are set free from demonic oppression and those who are unsaved can be set free from demonic possession.

> [17] Then one of the crowd answered and said, "Teacher, I brought You my son, who has a mute spirit. [18] And wherever it seizes him, it throws him down; he foams at the mouth, gnashes his teeth, and becomes rigid. So I spoke to Your disciples, that they should cast it out, but they could not."
> [19] He answered him and said, "O faithless generation, how long shall I be with you? How long shall I bear with you? Bring him to Me." [20] Then they brought him to Him. And when he saw Him, immediately the

spirit convulsed him, and he fell on the ground and wallowed, foaming at the mouth.

[21] So He asked his father, "How long has this been happening to him?"

And he said, "From childhood. [22] And often he has thrown him both into the fire and into the water to destroy him. But if You can do anything, have compassion on us and help us."

[23] Jesus said to him, "If you can believe, all things *are* possible to him who believes."

[24] Immediately the father of the child cried out and said with tears, "Lord, I believe; help my unbelief!"

[25] When Jesus saw that the people came running together, He rebuked the unclean spirit, saying to it: "Deaf and dumb spirit, I command you, come out of him and enter him no more!" [26] Then *the spirit* cried out, convulsed him greatly, and came out of him. And he became as one dead, so that many said, "He is dead." [27] But Jesus took him by the hand and lifted him up, and he arose.

[28] And when He had come into the house, His disciples asked Him privately, "Why could we not cast it out?"

[29] So He said to them, "This kind can come out by nothing but prayer and fasting," (Mark 9:17-29).

The Lord lived a constant life of fasting and praying. So much so, the disciples even became concerned about his lack of eating.

[30] Then they went out of the city and came to Him.

[31] In the meantime His disciples urged Him, saying, "Rabbi, eat."

[32] But He said to them, "I have food to eat of which you do not know."

[33] Therefore the disciples said to one another, "Has anyone brought Him *anything* to eat?"

> [34] Jesus said to them, "My food is to do the will of
> Him who sent Me, and to finish His work,
> (John 4:30-34 New King James Version).

Gluttony in America is a real issue. Food is available twenty-four hours a day, seven days a week, and it is the food that many consume that cause health problems. There have been testimonials people have shared of the benefits for losing weight. Many have clearer thinking, more energy, and even being told by their physician the need for high blood pressure medication was no longer needed all as a result of fasting and praying. Our bodies are the temple of the Holy Spirit.

> [19] What? know ye not that your body is the temple
> of the Holy Ghost which is in you, which ye have of
> God, and ye are not your own?
> [20] For ye are bought with a price: therefore glorify God
> in your body, and in your spirit, which are God's,
> (1 Corinthians 6:19-20).

The Lord's presence is no longer dwelling in tents, tabernacles or arks. The Lord dwells in us! When we accept Christ Jesus as our Lord and Savior, darkness is moved out and the Light moves in, hallelujah!

When fasting, it is good to have scriptures you believe God for in faith. Again, abstaining from food means to read the Bible, pray, and seek the Lord. People have shared how their attitudes and temperaments changed for the better as a result of living a fasted lifestyle. Be sensitive to the Holy Spirit. Ask Him about the duration of the fast and the type of fast He wants you to complete. There are times you might be so committed to fasting for an extended period of time and the Holy Spirit might even prompt you to end your fast early. Upon the conclusion of your fast, always end it with praise and worship. Fasting is a powerful spiritual weapon against satan and demonic forces as it pulls down strongholds as you become equipped to walk in the victory already given to you by the Lord.

Spiritual Weapon #4 Tithes and Offerings

For years, I would read the scriptures in Malachi about the tithes and offerings, however for years I would ask the Lord what was He really trying to convey to us in scripture?

> [8] Will a man rob **God?** Yet ye have robbed me. But ye say, Wherein have we robbed thee? In tithes and offerings.
> [9] Ye are cursed with a curse: for ye have robbed me, even this whole nation.
> [10] Bring ye all the tithes into the storehouse, that there may be meat in mine house, and prove me now herewith, saith **the LORD of hosts**, if I will not open you the windows of heaven, and pour you out a blessing, that there shall not be room enough to receive it.
> [11] And I will rebuke the devourer for your sakes, and he shall not destroy the fruits of your ground; neither shall your vine cast her fruit before the time in the field, **saith the LORD of hosts**.
> [12] And all nations shall call you blessed: for ye shall be a delightsome land, saith **the LORD of hosts.**
> [13] Your words have been stout against me, saith **the LORD.** Yet ye say, What have we spoken so much against thee? (Malachi 3:8-13 King James Version bold added for emphasis).

In verse eight the question is asked, "will a man rob God?" Therefore from verses eight through thirteen, we read God, the Lord of Hosts, and Lord. Verse thirteen is not a part of the context for the tithes, however for the sake of emphasis this verse is included. God, the Lord of Hosts, and Lord are some of the names to describe the attributes of the great I Am. The word God in verse eight is the Hebrew word elohiym which is defined as rulers, judges, divine ones, the (true) God. This is plural which is indicative of the Godhead. (Colossians 2:9 refers to the Godhead; and the Godhead is God:

Father, Son, and Holy Spirit). Therefore will a man or woman rob the Godhead is the initial question with Elohiym giving the answer of people robbing Him in their tithes and offerings.

Next we read "says the Lord of Hosts." The Lord of Hosts is a military term! I received the revelation of our tithes and offerings being a spiritual weapon against satan himself in Bible Study on a Wednesday night. Pastor Samuel Rodriguez wasn't even teaching on this scripture. He was teaching on something totally different, however he referenced the Lord of Hosts saying that means Jehovah Sabaoth which is defined as the Lord of the Angel Armies. I became so excited I exclaimed within myself, "THAT'S IT! THAT'S WHAT THAT MEANS!" I had become so excited that I zoned out of the rest of Bible Study excited that I finally received the answer to my question! (Sorry Pastor Samuel-slight chuckle)

And then in verse thirteen, the Lord brings rebuke for another area and the words, "says the Lord" are used.

In these scriptures on tithes and offerings for many, they would hear the emphasis preached or taught on being cursed with a curse. Well, thank you Jesus, we have been redeemed from the curse of the law.

> [13] Christ hath redeemed us from the curse of the law, being made a curse for us: for it is written, Cursed is every one that hangs on a tree, (Galatians 3:13). Therefore the emphasis is not on the curse, but rather being OBEDIENT to God. He told us to bring our tithes and offerings into the storehouse for the specific purpose of meat being in His house, or provision, and we can prove Him in this! Not many times in scripture does the Lord of Hosts tell us we can prove Him! But here He does. We can prove Him or put Him to the test to open the windows (that's plural) of Heaven and pour out a blessing so big there will not be enough room to receive it! But it doesn't stop there, glory to God. The Lord of Hosts will rebuke the devourer for our sakes. The devourer will not destroy the fruit

of our ground. And the Lord of Hosts still isn't finished! He goes on to say that ALL nations will call us blessed and we shall be a delightsome land.

Therefore, as you read this, you might be wondering, how is it then that the ten percent of our gross income plus our offerings is a spiritual weapon against satan? Good question!

> [8] Be sober, be vigilant; because your adversary the devil, as a roaring lion, walketh about, seeking whom he may **devour,** (1 Peter 5:8 King James Version-bold added for emphasis). Again, in the Old Testament, the children of Israel were only aware of natural enemies, however in the New Testament we are aware of spiritual enemies.

As we know our Great Lord, Master, and King, Christ Jesus is the Lion of the Tribe of Judah, (Revelation 5:5). Satan is a counterfeit. He cannot create therefore he will only try to duplicate but his duplication is deception and a lie. He is the father of lies, (John 8:44) Therefore, the Apostle Peter informs us that satan is on the prowl as a roaring lion seeking to devour. If satan is seeking to devour, then that means everyone cannot be devoured.

So here it is-EVERYTIME we bring the Lord of Hosts our tithes and offerings, we can expect Him as the Lord of the Angel Armies to go forth on our behalf and rebuke satan from every area of our lives! The Lord of Hosts, the Lord of the Angel Armies rebukes the devourer for us! Satan is attempting to devour more than just a person's finances. It is his wicked, evil, diabolical scheme to devour every area of a person's life. When we give the Lord His tenth plus offerings, we have a right to be excited and to say, "Jehovah Sabaoth, I prove you now to open the windows of heaven to bless me! I expect you to lead the charge against the devourer and rebuke him from every area of my life! I expect no premature blessings. I expect the fullness of my blessings and for others to see me blessed by you and to call me blessed! In Jesus name amen!"

What I love about this scripture is that the Lord of Hosts, Jehovah Sabaoth Himself is leading the charge against satan and his demons, hallelujah! The Lord is leading the charge, not Michael the archangel, not Gabriel the messenger angel, not one of the ministering angels, or any of the angelic hosts but rather it is the Lord!

Hence we come back to Revelation to read what this looks like!

> [11] And I saw heaven opened, and behold a white horse; and he that sat upon him was called Faithful and True, and in righteousness he does judge and make war.
> [12] His eyes were as a flame of fire, and on his head were many crowns; and he had a name written, that no man knew, but he himself.
> [13] And he was clothed with a vesture dipped in blood: and his name is called **The Word of God.**
> [14] **And the armies which were in heaven followed him upon white horses**, clothed in fine linen, white and clean.
> [15] **And out of his mouth goes a sharp sword**, that with it he should smite the nations: and he shall rule them with a rod of iron: and he treads the winepress of the fierceness and wrath of Almighty God.
> [16] And he hath on his vesture and on his thigh a name written, KING OF KINGS, AND LORD OF LORDS
> (Revelation 19:11-16 bold added for emphasis).

Although this is the Apostle John writing about the great honor and privilege of the Lord revealing to him about the end time, our Great Lord is not a Lamb anymore! He had to become the Lamb of God to die for our sins. Salvation and redemption are available through His blood. He is high and lifted up seated on His throne! Glory to God! And He is making intercession for us, but that will be discussed later in further detail.

Again, we see Jesus, who is the Word of God, leading the charge with His angelic armies following Him! In Malachi, the Lord of Hosts is stated three times from verses eight through thirteen. For the Lord to repeat Himself several times, He is emphasizing His military position. The tithes and offerings are a spiritual weapon against satan and his demonic spirits because Jehovah Sabaoth is rebuking him, thank you Lord Jesus! Therefore, stop saying you need to "pay" tithes. God is not a bill. He is not a debt. We cannot buy a blessing. All He is asking for is ten percent. What is ten percent when He in turn blesses that tenth with so much more?

Of course there are those who want to argue that tithing is under the law. Not true. The Lord made His covenant with Abraham, and Abraham gave tithes to King Melchizedek. This covenant was made before the Law of Moses.

> [18] And Melchizedek king of Salem brought forth bread and wine: and he was the priest of the most high God. [19] And he blessed him, and said, Blessed be Abram of the most high God, possessor of heaven and earth: [20] And blessed be the most high God, which hath delivered thine enemies into thy hand. And he gave him tithes of all (Genesis 14:18-20). Notice the tithe occurred prior to the Lord changing Abraham's name from Abram.

For this Melchisedec, king of Salem, priest of the most high God, who met Abraham returning from the slaughter of the kings, and blessed him;

> [2] To whom also Abraham gave a tenth part of all; first being by interpretation King of righteousness, and after that also King of Salem, which is, King of peace; [3] Without father, without mother, without descent, having neither beginning of days, nor end of life; but made like unto the Son of God; abideth a priest continually. [4] Now consider how great this man was, unto whom even the patriarch Abraham gave the tenth of the spoils.

⁵ And verily they that are of the sons of Levi, who receive the office of the priesthood, have a commandment to take tithes of the people according to the law, that is, of their brethren, though they come out of the loins of Abraham:
⁶ But he whose descent is not counted from them received tithes of Abraham, and blessed him that had the promises.
⁷ And without all contradiction the less is blessed of the better.
⁸ And here men that die receive tithes; but there he receiveth them, of whom it is witnessed that he liveth.
⁹ And as I may so say, Levi also, who receiveth tithes, payed tithes in Abraham.
¹⁰ For he was yet in the loins of his father, when Melchisedec met him   (Hebrews 7:1-10).

Now our Lord and Savior is our Great High Priest after the order of Melchisedec.

⁵ So also Christ glorified not himself to be made an high priest; but he that said unto him, Thou art my Son, to day have I begotten thee.
⁶ As he saith also in another place, Thou art a priest for ever after the order of Melchisedec, (Hebrews 5:5-6).

Read Hebrews chapters five, six, seven, and eight. These scriptures will confirm what happened in the Old Testament is still relevant in the New Covenant. We still present our tithes to our High Priest, Christ Jesus by bringing them to church. Now some ask the question do we tithe on gross or net? My answer to this is, when applying for a car loan or a home loan; do you provide your net income or your gross income? So why would we cheat the Lord out of His tithe by giving Him what's His after Uncle Sam and taxes get theirs? The Lord is always priority so give Him His tenth on your gross. You must not say you cannot afford it, because truth is you cannot afford not to. Again, this is a spiritual weapon against the adversary for we see in scripture our Lord personally leads the charge to rebuke the devourer, hallelujah!

Spiritual Weapon #5 Prayer

There are many types of prayers that we as Believers are to pray to obtain different victorious results for every area of our lives. The prayer of Binding and Loosing, prayer of Agreement, prayer of Intercession, praying in tongues, prayer of Supplication, prayer of Faith, prayer of Dedication and Consecration, and the prayer of Thanksgiving are all power spiritual weapons that are a part of our Heavenly Arsenal. Our prayers do much damage to the forces of darkness.

The prayer of Binding and Loosing was introduced by our Lord and Savior. He said it is through this prayer that we have the keys of the Kingdom of Heaven.

> [19] And I will give unto thee the keys of the kingdom of heaven: and whatsoever you will bind on earth shall be bound in heaven: and whatsoever you will loose on earth shall be loosed in heaven, (Matthew 16:19).

The Lord repeated this again.

> [18] Verily I say unto you, Whatsoever you will bind on earth will be bound in heaven: and whatsoever you will loose on earth shall be loosed in heaven
> (Matthew 18:18).

Spiritual Weapon number 2 Praise and Worship, Psalm 149:8 states bind their kings with chains, and their nobles with fetters of iron. This is symbolic. Not binding people in the literal sense with chains and fetters of iron but rather demonic entities are bound. When the Lord came to the earth, He brought His power And authority and

He has delegated His power and authority to His Church over the powers of darkness.

In both scriptures in Matthew, the Greek word for bind is deh'o which means to be in bonds, knit, tie, wind and the word loose in the Greek is the word loo'o which means to break (up), destroy, dissolve, melt, put off. Now the word bind from Psalm 149:8, the Hebrew word means to join battle; bind fast, gird, harness, hold, keep, make ready, order, prepare, prison(-er), put in bonds, set in array, tie.

In the Old Testament, we have scripture where the children of Israel fought many battles and wars with no mention of dealing with demonic entities that they were aware of. Even when King David was tempted by satan to number Israel, (1 Chronicles 21:1), David was not aware of the demonic entity. David and many others in the Old Testament were aware of warring angels with their swords drawn (1 Chronicles 21:16).

When we as Christians bind and loose, the Word of our Lord is that all of Heaven is backing us. As we bind here Heaven is binding too, when we loose here Heaven is loosing also. Glory to God! Now, taking into consideration what the Greek word for loose is, takes on a new reality that for years the prayers of binding and loosing have not been prayed correctly. When this prayer is prayed, when we loose, what we are in essence saying is that we are commanding things to be broken up, destroyed, dissolved, melted, and put off. WOW! How many times have we bound lack and commanded our finances to be loosed? We no longer loose that which we need but rather we command what we need to be released in Jesus name.

Now the word bind is not limited to a negative connotation. It is defined as bonds, knit, tie, and wind in the Greek. Let's look at scriptures in the Hebrew as well.

> [3] Let not mercy and truth forsake thee: bind them about thy neck; write them upon the table of thine heart,   (Proverbs 3:3).

²Keep my commandments, and live; and my law as the apple of thine eye.

³Bind them upon thy fingers, write them upon the table of thine heart,   (Proverbs 7:2-3).

The Hebrew word for bind here is qashar, which is defined as tie, gird, confine, compact, bind (up), join together, knit. Therefore when praying the prayer of binding and loosing, we can bind that which is negative and demonic, and we can also bind to us what is needed.

If a person who is born again, yet living a wayward life, you can pray, "Lord according to your Word, you have given to me the keys of the Kingdom of Heaven. Therefore, I bind every demonic influence in (person's name) to be bound by being knit, tied and wound up, and now I loose those evil spirits and strongholds from (person's name) by being broken up, destroyed, dissolved, melted, and put off. I now bind the mind of Christ to (person's name), I bind the peace, the shalom of God to (person's life), I bind the love of Jesus to (person's life) now in the name of Jesus Christ of Nazareth. And I thank you Lord as I bind and loose here on earth, it is bound and loosed in Heaven and I thank you for it, in Jesus name I pray amen."

If you are praying for financial increase and you are sowing by giving and tithing, you still have the Kingdom authority to bind every spirit of lack, insufficiency, and delay in the name of Jesus. You have the right to live in the blessings of Abraham because of Jesus. Again, according to the Word, when we bind and loose, in the Greek loose is not releasing but actually dissolving, melting, destroying, breaking up, putting off. You have the keys to bind and loose and you have the keys to release, this is because of our Lord.

The example of prayer I provided comes from the Lord teaching on the strongman, (Matthew 12:29 and Mark 3:27). Remember, we wrestle not against flesh and blood. The life of the Believer is spiritual, it's supernatural. There are demonic entities at work to kill, steal, and destroy. Glory to God we have been given power and authority because of our Lord Jesus and nothing shall by any means hurt us! Thank you Jesus!

"The religion scholars from Jerusalem came down spreading rumors that he was working black magic, using devil tricks to impress them with spiritual power. Jesus confronted their slander with a story: "Does it make sense to send a devil to catch a devil, to use Satan to get rid of Satan? A constantly squabbling family disintegrates. If Satan were fighting Satan, there soon wouldn't be any Satan left. Do you think it's possible in broad daylight to enter the house of an awake, able-bodied man, and walk off with his possessions unless you tie him up first? Tie him up, though, and you can clean him out," (Mark 3:22-27 the Message Translation).

> [27] Satan must be bound before his demons are cast out,
> just as a strong man must be tied up before his house
> can be ransacked and his property robbed
> (Mark 3:27 the Living Bible).

In these passages of scripture, the Lord reveals that His Kingdom is here in the earth. The Kingdom of God has authority in the earth to tie up the powers of darkness. Ransacking satan's property by setting the captives free, healing the sick, raising the dead, opening deaf ears, restoring lives, etc. We have the anointing from the Lord to do these things.

When we bind the works of darkness, we can deploy our angels who are waiting for our command. Their assignment is to go forth and bind the works of darkness and to use chains to do so. This assignment is for the warring angels. An example of what this looks like in scripture is found in the book of Revelation.

And I saw an angel come down from heaven, having the key of the bottomless pit and a great chain in his hand.

> [2] And he laid hold on the dragon, that old serpent, which is the Devil, and Satan, and bound him a thousand years,
> [3] And cast him into the bottomless pit, and shut him up, and set a seal upon him, that he should deceive the nations no more, till the thousand years should

be fulfilled: and after that he must be loosed a little
season,   (Revelation 20:1-3).

Notice that ONE angel from heaven came and bound satan with a GREAT chain. There is no mention of a struggle or a fight, and satan did not call for back up to help him. This scripture reveals that the warring angels of the Lord are more powerful than satan himself.

Binding and Loosing Dream

I had a dream. I believe it was truly indicative of what binding and loosing looks like in the spirit realm.

In my dream, there was a huge winged demon that was flying overhead. In its claws it had an imp clutched in its grip holding it tightly. The imp resembled a monkey like creature. The demon dropped the imp into the backyard of a nice neighborhood. The imp was holding a bag and went into the backdoor of someone's home. It came out a short while later with the bag filled with nice possessions. The big winged demon clutched the imp and was taking flight. Suddenly, a warring angel with a huge sword in his hand came zooming down from heaven with lightening speed. His sword was lifted up high in one hand and a huge roped bag in his other hand. The warring angel knocked the demon out of the air with his sword. He bound the demon and the imp with the roped bag so fast that the imp dropped the bag with the possessions it had just stolen. At that moment, another warring angel came zooming down from heaven also with his sword lifted up high in the air. The big winged demon was extremely angry. Its wings were crushed inside the bag yet it used its claws to begin to attack the imp. The imp let out a loud shrill of pain. It was at that moment the first warring angel flew off with the demons and the second warring angel took the possessions that were stolen out of the home. He walked into the backdoor and restored everything back into its proper place as though nothing was taken. When the second warring angel's assignment was complete, he flew back upwards to heaven with his sword lifted up high in the air.

91

That dream really blessed me. I do not know where the first warring angel went with those demons. I thought about what the Lord said when satan was kicked out of heaven.

> [17] And the seventy returned again with joy, saying, Lord, even the devils are subject unto us through thy name.
> **[18] And he said unto them, I beheld Satan as lightning fall from heaven.**
> [19] Behold, I give unto you power to tread on serpents and scorpions, and over all the power of the enemy: and nothing shall by any means hurt you,
> (Luke 10:17-19 bold added for emphasis).

In other words, the Lord was saying to His seventy disciples that He watched satan fall so fast from Heaven it was a flash like lightening. The Lord WATCHED! He did not even participate in the battle. The angels of the Lord who did not follow Lucifer, fought against satan and the other fallen angels and it happened so fast. Now you can understand if the warring angels are that powerful against the kingdom of darkness, how much more powerful is our Lord against satan and his demonic hierarchy? There is no contest. Satan is NO match for our Lord. And the Lord Jesus has given every Believer power over the enemy and nothing shall by any means hurt us. Satan doesn't want Christians to know this. So what he does is he tries to amplify who he is.

When I was a child, I had to be in bed by a certain time. There were many nights I was restless as my sister and brother were able to stay up late. I didn't think this was fair for them to have all of the fun! There would be times I would use my hands to make shadow pictures from the light that was coming into my bedroom from the kitchen. I would make the face of a dog or a butterfly, to entertain myself until eventually I would fall off to sleep. And as small as my hands were, the shadow projected an image on the wall that looked bigger. That's what satan does. He tries to project images or amplify his lies to be bigger than what they are.

In fact, the Word of God reveals to us, that people will be shocked when satan's true identity is revealed.

> ¹⁶ They that see thee shall narrowly look upon thee, and consider thee, saying, Is this the man that made the earth to tremble, that did shake kingdoms;
> ¹⁷ That made the world as a wilderness, and destroyed the cities thereof; that opened not the house of his prisoners?
> ¹⁸ All the kings of the nations, even all of them, lie in glory, every one in his own house.
> ¹⁹ But thou art cast out of thy grave like an abominable branch, and as the raiment of those that are slain, thrust through with a sword, that go down to the stones of the pit; as a carcase trodden under feet.
> ²⁰ Thou shalt not be joined with them in burial, because thou hast destroyed thy land, and slain thy people: the seed of evildoers shall never be renowned.
>
> (Isaiah 14:16-20)

People are going to have the attitude of no way! Not him! Is this the one who did all of this damage in the earth and to people's lives? Remember, satan has already been defeated by our Great Lord, Jesus the Christ!

Now I'm sure by now you might be asking yourself the question, what about the Prophet Daniel when his prayer was held up for twenty-one days?

> ⁷ And I Daniel alone saw the vision: for the men that were with me saw not the vision; but a great quaking fell upon them, so that they fled to hide themselves.
> ⁸ Therefore I was left alone, and saw this great vision, and there remained no strength in me: for my comeliness was turned in me into corruption, and I retained no strength.

⁹Yet heard I the voice of his words: and when I heard the voice of his words, then was I in a deep sleep on my face, and my face toward the ground.

¹⁰And, behold, an hand touched me, which set me upon my knees and upon the palms of my hands.

¹¹And he said unto me, O Daniel, a man greatly beloved, understand the words that I speak unto thee, and stand upright: for unto thee am I now sent. And when he had spoken this word unto me, I stood trembling.

¹²Then said he unto me, Fear not, Daniel: for from the first day that you did set your heart to understand, and to chasten yourself before your God, your words were heard, and I am come for your words.

¹³But the prince of the kingdom of Persia withstood me one and twenty days: but, lo, Michael, **one of the chief princes**, came to help me; and I remained there with the kings of Persia

(Daniel 10:7-13 bold added for emphasis).

The angel of the Lord was sent to Daniel to give him revelation of things to come. The demonic spirit assigned to that region hindered the angel. HOWEVER, Michael ONE OF THE CHIEF PRINCES in the Lord's angelic rank was sent to help the first angel so his mission to Daniel could be accomplished. Daniel did not have the authority in the Old Covenant to bind and loose. But notice here what the angel told him. "Your words were heard, and I am come for your WORDS," (capitalization added for emphasis). So it is for us in this spiritual warfare, the angels of the Lord can only respond to our words that are based on the Word of God. We deploy our angels by saying it is written. We deploy our angels by saying what the Word of God says. Our angels do not respond to murmuring, complaining, or words of doubt, skepticism, or unbelief. This is why we must spend time reading our Bibles to know the language of Heaven so our angels can respond accordingly.

In Proverbs, we read where we are to bind the Lord's commandments and His mercy and truth around our necks and around our fingers. This is a good binding. I often pray I bind the love of Jesus to my heart. I bind the peace which is the shalom of God to my thoughts. I bind the Lord's health and healing to my mind and my emotions in the name of Jesus Christ. Yes the Lord's love has been shed abroad in our hearts by the Holy Spirit (Romans 5:5), however it still serves as a reminder to walk in the love of God towards everyone as the Lord commands.

When the prayer of Binding and Loosing is prayed, that is definitely a spiritual military attack against the kingdom of darkness. Our prayers cause a violent attack against satan and his demons, thank you Jesus! We must bind and loose to recapture that which was stolen. Picture this: when our Navy Seals have been given orders to go on a classified hostile and dangerous assignment to go into another country and release hostages, whether American or allies, they are going in to assess the situation, identify the targets, remove the threats and rescue the hostages releasing them to safety and getting them from harm's way. Our prayers of binding and loosing do the same thing! Remember, when we bind and loose, all of Heaven is backing us!

Here is a biblical example of that analogy. Real life search and rescue in the Bible.

> ³ So David and his men came to the city, and, behold, it was burned with fire; and their wives, and their sons, and their daughters, were taken captives.
> ⁴ Then David and the people that were with him lifted up their voice and wept, until they had no more power to weep.
> ⁵ And David's two wives were taken captives, Ahinoam the Jezreelitess, and Abigail the wife of Nabal the Carmelite.
> ⁶ And David was greatly distressed; for the people spake of stoning him, because the soul of all the people was grieved, every man for his sons and for

his daughters: but David encouraged himself in the
Lord his God.

⁷And David said to Abiathar the priest, Ahimelech's
son, I pray thee, bring me hither the ephod. And
Abiathar brought thither the ephod to David.

⁸And David enquired at the Lord, saying, Shall I
pursue after this troop? shall I overtake them? And he
answered him, Pursue: for thou shalt surely overtake
them, and without fail recover all (1 Samuel 30:3-8).

This is so powerful! King David was a man of war; however he
had a very close relationship with the Lord. EVERYTHING was
taken not only from him but from all of the men who were with
him. Consider the honorable thing David did. He encouraged himself
in the Lord! He cried and wept sorely with the others. Even when
the other men spoke of stoning him, he did not become combative
towards them, but rather HE SOUGHT THE LORD! Hallelujah!
He asked the Lord, should I pursue after them? Should I overtake
them? The Lord answered him that he would not only pursue after
the enemy, but that he will SURELY overtake them AND without
fail recover ALL! That is powerful!

We as Christians should not only pursue what satan had stolen
from us, but with the power and the anointing from the Lord we are
equipped to overtake and to recover all! Thank you Jesus!

³The Lord is a man of war: the Lord is his name, (Exodus 15:3).
When satan is doing everything he can to steal from
you; steal your dreams, steal your vision, steal your
money, kill your goals, destroy your family, destroy
your marriage, destroy your health, etc., child of God
that is when you need to gird up with strength and
encourage yourself in the Lord! Seek the Lord and
begin to use the keys of the Kingdom of Heaven
against that defeated foe in the name of Jesus! Pursue,
overtake, and recover it all in the name of Jesus!

[12] And from the time John the Baptist began preaching
until now, the Kingdom of Heaven has been force-
fully advancing, and violent people are attacking it,
            (Matthew 11:12 New Living Translation).

This is why it is imperative for every Christian to know that we
are all drafted into the army of the Lord as it were. We win because
Jesus has already defeated satan hallelujah!

[19] Behold, I give unto you power to tread on serpents
and scorpions, and over all the power of the enemy:
and **nothing** shall by any means hurt you,
            (Luke 10:19 bold added for emphasis).

This is why Christianity cannot be perceived as cotton candy,
where we just go through life living in a bubble, or our heads buried
in the sand like an ostrich trying to hide. Not wanting to face and
overcome real life issues, living almost delusional with no account-
ability or no reference to reality but almost a superficial notion of 'all
I have to do is quote scripture, live by faith, and everything is going
to work out is not the reality of Christianity. The reality is we all
have a real adversary who hates, despises and detests EVERYONE,
not just us Christians.

We were created in the image and likeness of God, (Genesis 1:26).
Even as strong and powerful as Michael the archangel is, he was
NOT created in the image and likeness of God. That's why people
need to stop saying about people who have died, or as the Bible calls
it fell asleep, (1 Thessalonians 4:13-18) to stop saying they earned
their wings because they're not in the image of angels but in the
image and likeness of God. We don't earn wings. We will receive a
glorified body (Philippians 3:21).

The bottom-line, it doesn't matter if you go to church weekly and
hold your Bible in the air. If you never open it to read it, then what
was gained? What did you learn? How is your mind renewed? Faith
comes by hearing the Word, yet we must also read the Word. Reading
the Word of God feeds our spirit and causes us to grow spiritually.

As previously stated from Spiritual Weapon #1 which is the Word of God, the Word of God is Jesus, and that is why satan is working so hard to keep Christians from reading their Bibles. The Word is our Sword which we use against satan and his demons.

Putting the Bible under your pillow won't stop you from having nightmares either. The reality is there are people reading this book right now, who have encountered demonic entities in their home or on their jobs; seeing shadows, hearing voices, being attacked at night, not able to move, etc. Jesus Christ is Lord and the Lord is Greater than all of those demonic attacks, so right now in the name of Jesus I set myself in agreement with you and Father I bind every satanic demonic attack of night terrors, nightmares, bad dreams, shadows, ghosts, and every other diabolical entity to be bound right now in the name of Jesus Christ of Nazareth. And Lord I call forth a legion of warring angels with their swords drawn to go forth and do battle right now on behalf of every person reading this. Warring angels as those evil spirits are bound in Jesus name I command them to be loosed and cast out of the home or job of the person reading this and cast them back into the pits of hell. I cover their thought life, their dream life, their homes, and their work with the Blood of Jesus right now. Lord, bless their dreams, bless their thoughts. I bind the mind of Christ to their minds right now reading this and I thank you Lord for releasing your great power in their lives, in their homes, and on their jobs now in the name of Jesus. I bind and I rebuke the spirit of fear and I command that fear to be loosed from them right now and cast back into the pits of hell. Glory to God! I thank you Lord that you have given to them your power, your love, and your sound mind. It is in Jesus name that I pray and ask this and now Lord I rebuke backlash, retaliation, and revenge from the adversary and I cancel every demonic assignment. It is in the all powerful name of Jesus I pray, amen and so be it! Hallelujah!

Now begin to worship the Lord and thank Him for restoring back unto you EVERYTHING the adversary stole from you. It is time for you to have life and have it more abundantly because of the Lord (John 10:10).

Now this is the reason we NEVER pray binding satan's power over a person, church, event, job etc. That's an incorrect prayer. We command satan's power to be loosed off people's lives, churches, events, jobs, etc. We ask the Lord to release His power over a person, church, event, job, etc.

This is what spiritual warfare is all about. Not focusing on the defeated demonic, but looking to Jesus for His mighty power to manifest. That's spiritual warfare! Removing the target and gaining ground advancing the Kingdom of God.

The Prayer of Agreement

> [19] Again I say unto you, That if two of you shall agree on earth as touching any thing that they shall ask, it shall be done for them of my Father which is in heaven. [20] For where two or three are gathered together in my name, there am I in the midst of them (Matthew 18:19-20).
>
> [18-20] "Take this most seriously: A yes on earth is yes in heaven; a no on earth is no in heaven. What you say to one another is eternal. I mean this. When two of you get together on anything at all on earth and make a prayer of it, my Father in heaven goes into action. And when two or three of you are together because of me, you can be sure that I'll be there."
>
> (Matthew 18:18-20 the Message Translation).

The prayer of agreement is a powerful spiritual weapon against the adversary. In scripture we read where the Lord sent out his disciples two by two, (Mark 6:7, Luke 10:1). One of my favorite sayings I like to use when I contact one of my prayer partners is, "Cover me I'm going in!" Ahhh I love it! This is my way of saying to my prayer partner, please come into agreement with me. Even law enforcement calls for backup. Why do some Christians go through life as though they're super saints and do not need anyone to pray with them in agreement?

> [9] Two are better than one; because they have a good
> reward for their labour.
> [10] For if they fall, the one will lift up his fellow: but
> woe to him that is alone when he falleth; for he hath
> not another to help him up.
> [11] Again, if two lie together, then they have heat: but
> how can one be warm alone?
> [12] And if one prevail against him, two shall withstand
> him; and a threefold cord is not quickly broken.
> (Ecclesiastes 4:9-12).

All throughout scriptures from the Old to the New Testament, metaphors are used. Such metaphors are descriptors for people's behavior or character, i.e. wolves in sheep clothing, goats, lamp, sheep, swine, and dogs. As a child, I grew up watching animal programs with my dad. Even now as an adult, I still enjoy watching animal programs with my husband. One of the things that is so amazing about predator and prey is the commonality of separation and isolation. From the Orcas or killer whales in the ocean, bald eagles in the air, or lions in the jungles of Africa, these predators in search for food go after the prey that's been separated from the rest of the group. Why is this? Because even the animals recognize there's strength in numbers. As previously stated 1 Peter 5:8 teaches us our adversary the devil is as a roaring lion seeking to devour.

The prayer of agreement provides spiritual backup and reinforcement. There are times spiritual warfare might become so intense the need for spiritual support is dire. And this is perfectly fine. Do not allow the lies of satan make you feel as though you're not good enough or not strong enough, or not deep enough spiritually to handle all of life's situations by yourself.

> [30] How should one chase a thousand, and two put ten
> thousand to flight, except their Rock had sold them,
> and the LORD had shut them up? (Deuteronomy 32:30).

When we come into agreement, the Word of God teaches us one can chase a thousand and two can put ten thousand to flight. This is only because our Rock, Christ Jesus has given us the power to do so. The Lord said as we are gathered together in His name He is in our midst. He is with us. As previously stated, King David sought the Lord and the Lord let him know that he will pursue, he will overtake, and he will recover all because the Lord was with him.

How many Christians today are trying to pursue dreams, or recover from a setback without seeking the Lord first? Oftentimes people consult with each other and get advice from other's rather than seeking the Lord. Why do so many Christians seek the Lord as a last resort rather than a first priority?

The prayer of agreement is a powerful spiritual weapon against the adversary because very few people are needed to bring destruction to his plans. No need to be discouraged when the attendance for the prayer meetings are low. It's best to have five who are truly in agreement rather than to have a hundred who are not in agreement. Some can say amen with their words yet be in doubt and unbelief with their hearts.

The Lord chose twelve disciples, yet throughout the Gospels, we read where Peter, James, and John were chosen to be with the Lord the most.

> [35] While He was still speaking, *some* came from the ruler of the synagogue's *house* who said, "Your daughter is dead. Why trouble the Teacher any further?" [36] As soon as Jesus heard the word that was spoken, He said to the ruler of the synagogue, "Do not be afraid; only believe." [37] And He permitted no one to follow Him except Peter, James, and John the brother of James. [38] Then He came to the house of the ruler of the synagogue, and saw a tumult and those who wept and wailed loudly. [39] When He came in, He said to them, "Why make this commotion and weep? The child is not dead, but sleeping."

⁴⁰ And they ridiculed Him. But when He had put them all outside, He took the father and the mother of the child, and those *who were* with Him, and entered where the child was lying. ⁴¹ Then He took the child by the hand, and said to her, "Talitha, cumi," which is translated, "Little girl, I say to you, arise." ⁴² Immediately the girl arose and walked, for she was twelve years *of age*. And they were overcome with great amazement.

(Mark 5:35-42 New King James Version)

When praying the prayer of agreement, it is imperative to have someone with equal faith or greater faith than yours. In other words, a Sergeant will not go to a private. A General will not go to a Sergeant. The private goes to the Sergeant and the Sergeant goes to the General because of the higher rank of authority and experience. There are baby Christians who are referred to as lamb who need to be able to go to the sheep. The sheep are the more mature Christians. Lamb are on the milk of the Word and sheep are on the meat of the Word.

The Prayer of Intercession

The prayer of intercession is another powerful spiritual weapon against the adversary. Interceding on behalf of another or what is also referred to as standing in the gap is powerful. There are times when people go to the altar at church and request prayer for someone who is not present is referred to as standing "in proxy" for the person.

"And I sought for a man among them, that should make up the hedge, and stand in the gap before me for the land, that I should not destroy it: but I found none," (Ezekiel 22:30).

Both Abraham and Moses are referred to as being a friend of God (James 2:23, Exodus 33:11). What an honor and a blessing to be called a friend of God Almighty! The good news is, the Lord said in His Word He no longer calls us servants but He calls us friends, (John 15:15). What a blessing, an honor, and a privilege for the King of Glory to desire to speak with us, and commune with us as friends. Friends are aware of close, personal, private, and privy information. This is why the Lord will awaken His sons and daughters at early morning hours just to talk.

Abraham was an intercessor for his nephew Lot. The Lord revealed to Abraham His plans to destroy the wicked and abominable places of Sodom and Gomorrah.

> [16] And the men rose up from thence, and looked toward Sodom: and Abraham went with them to bring them on the way.
>
> [17] And the LORD said, Shall I hide from Abraham that thing which I do;
>
> [18] Seeing that Abraham shall surely become a great and mighty nation, and all the nations of the earth shall be blessed in him?
>
> [19] For I know him, that he will command his children and his household after him, and they shall keep the way of the LORD, to do justice and judgment; that the LORD may bring upon Abraham that which he hath spoken of him.
>
> [20] And the LORD said, Because the cry of Sodom and Gomorrah is great, and because their sin is very grievous;
>
> [21] I will go down now, and see whether they have done altogether according to the cry of it, which is come unto me; and if not, I will know.
>
> [22] And the men turned their faces from thence, and went toward Sodom: but Abraham stood yet before the LORD.
>
> [23] And Abraham drew near, and said, Wilt thou also destroy the righteous with the wicked?

²⁴ Peradventure there be fifty righteous within the city: wilt thou also destroy and not spare the place for the fifty righteous that are therein?

²⁵ That be far from thee to do after this manner, to slay the righteous with the wicked: and that the righteous should be as the wicked, that be far from thee: Shall not the Judge of all the earth do right?

²⁶ And the LORD said, If I find in Sodom fifty righteous within the city, then I will spare all the place for their sakes.

²⁷ And Abraham answered and said, Behold now, I have taken upon me to speak unto the LORD, which am but dust and ashes:

²⁸ Peradventure there shall lack five of the fifty righteous: wilt thou destroy all the city for lack of five? And he said, If I find there forty and five, I will not destroy it.

²⁹ And he spake unto him yet again, and said, Peradventure there shall be forty found there. And he said, I will not do it for forty's sake.

³⁰ And he said unto him, Oh let not the LORD be angry, and I will speak: Peradventure there shall thirty be found there. And he said, I will not do it, if I find thirty there.

³¹ And he said, Behold now, I have taken upon me to speak unto the LORD: Peradventure there shall be twenty found there. And he said, I will not destroy it for twenty's sake.

³² And he said, Oh let not the LORD be angry, and I will speak yet but this once: Peradventure ten shall be found there. And he said, I will not destroy it for ten's sake.

³³ And the LORD went his way, as soon as he had left communing with Abraham: and Abraham returned unto his place.   (Genesis 18:16-33).

The prayer of intercession is continual. It is not the same as the prayer of faith. Intercession is the continual standing in the gap for a person's deliverance; from danger, death, strongholds in the form of alcohol, drugs, gambling, etc. The prayer of intercession is a powerful spiritual weapon against the adversary as it is not the Lord's will for any to perish but for all to come to repentance, (2 Peter 3:9).

Usually when there is a burden on one's heart (spiritually not physically), or an inner knowing of something is not right, do not overlook this or push past it. That is the prompting of the Holy Spirit to begin to pray. Our prayers give Kingdom access in this earth realm to continue to foil and destroy the plans and works of darkness.

Intercession is necessary for unsaved family members, loved ones, co-workers, etc.

> "In whom the god of this world hath blinded the minds of them which believe not, lest the light of the glorious gospel of Christ, who is the image of God, should shine unto them," (2 Corinthians 4:4).

The Word of God refers to satan as the god of this world. This scripture teaches us as Christians that his works are to blind the minds of people who do not believe unless the light of the glorious gospel of our Lord should shine to them.

"For the god of this world has blinded the unbelievers' minds [that they should not discern the truth], preventing them from seeing the illuminating light of the Gospel of the glory of Christ (the Messiah), Who is the Image *and* Likeness of God," (2 Corinthians 4:4 Amplified Version).

When we pray for others by way of intercession, we are commanding the forces of darkness to be loosed from their minds and we can command the light of the Gospel and glory of the Anointed One to shine forth into their minds. For people who are born-again yet living wayward lives, we can intercede binding the mind of Christ to their minds, (Philippians 2:5).

When you pray the prayer of intercession you can also "deploy" or send forth the ministering angels and ministering spirits to the person or people you're praying for.

> "Are not the angels all ministering spirits (servants) sent out in the service [of God for the assistance] of those who are to inherit salvation?"
> (Hebrews 1:14 Amplified Version).

In essence, all Christians are called to intercede. There are those who have a heart and a burden to pray continuously for people, hours at a time. They are given a grace from the Lord to be able to do so. However, all Christians need to stand in the gap for souls. It is the adversary's desire to keep as many in darkness as possible. Prayers of intercession cause that darkness to be removed. Thank you Lord Jesus!

Praying in Tongues (Heavenly Prayer Language)

Allow me to preface this part that praying in tongues, is receiving the baptism of the Holy Ghost (Luke 3:16, Acts 1:5), and is not the same as the gift of tongues described in 1 Corinthians chapters 12 and 14). These are two separate functions by the Holy Spirit for different purposes. I'm specifically referring to what our Lord said about us to be endued with power from on high.

> "And, behold, I send the promise of my Father upon you: but tarry ye in the city of Jerusalem, until ye be endued with power from on high,"   (Luke 24:49).

The promise from the Heavenly Father has come. John spoke that we will be baptized with the Holy Spirit and fire.

> "I indeed baptize you with water unto repentance: but he that cometh after me is mightier than I, whose

shoes I am not worthy to bear: he shall baptize you with the Holy Ghost, and with fire:" (Matthew 3:11).

And when the day of Pentecost was fully come, they were all with one accord in one place.

> [2] And suddenly there came a sound from heaven as of a rushing mighty wind, and it filled all the house where they were sitting.
> [3] And there appeared unto them cloven **tongues like as of fire,** and it sat upon each of them.
> [4] **And they were all filled with the Holy Ghost, and began to speak with other tongues, as the Spirit gave them utterance.**
> (Acts 2:1-4 bold added for emphasis).

The promise has come! Speaking in tongues is the most powerful prayer weapon in our heavenly arsenal.

Years ago, the military used a form of communication called Morse code. That communication used a series of clicks, and tones using special equipment. That code is now obsolete as the military uses highly sophisticated and classified forms of communication. Praying in tongues is the highest classified form of heavenly communication for Christians. When we pray in our native birth language, whether it is English, Japanese, Spanish, French, or a dialect from the Philippine Islands, Africa, etc. that communication in prayer is limited. Praying in tongues is a prayer language that can never be intercepted by enemy forces from the kingdom of darkness.

> "Likewise the Spirit also helps in our weaknesses. For we do not know what we should pray for as we ought, but the Spirit Himself makes intercession for us with groanings which cannot be uttered," (Romans 8:26).

This scripture clearly teaches us there are times in life when we to pray to our Heavenly Father that we cannot even put the words together to articulate what we need or desire to receive from Him. Therefore when we begin to pray in tongues, pray in our Heavenly language, that is the highest form of communication because the Holy Spirit makes intercession for us! Isn't that powerful?! We are not alone. The Holy Spirit is here as our Comforter and Intercessor!

Our Lord Jesus is also making intercession for us!

> "Who is he that condemns? It is Christ that died, yea rather, that is risen again, who is even at the right hand of God, who also makes intercession for us,"
> (Romans 8:34).

What a blessing and a comfort in knowing that God the Son and God the Holy Spirit are making intercession for us!

Therefore when we pray in our Heavenly prayer language, satan nor his demons, cannot infiltrate, hinder, stop, or block such prayers because it is a language given to us by the Holy Spirit. Satan does not know all things. This prayer is the supernatural power of God. Our spirit commune with the Godhead and in turn the Holy Spirit fills our spirit with revelation about any given situation. He gives us wisdom, knowledge and understanding. You can pray in tongues anywhere; at home, in your car, on the airplane, at work, etc. And you do not have to lift up your voice really loud to do so either. Remember, the Holy Spirit is referred to as the still small voice, (1 Kings 19:12). This is why those who are not born-again will refer to Him as "something told me" or "I should have followed my first mind." The Holy Spirit is gentle and He is the one who is the conscious for the world and convincer and convicter and conscience for the Saints.

Speaking in tongues also builds us up.

> "But you, beloved, building up yourselves on your most holy faith, praying in the Holy Ghost,"   (Jude 1:20).

In essence, the powerful spiritual weapon of speaking in tongues also referred to as praying in the Holy Ghost, praying in the Spirit, praying in our Heavenly prayer language, are all synonymous with the evidence of Holy Ghost baptism. The Holy Spirit gives the utterance. It is a divine language to communicate with the Father on behalf of others as well as for ourselves.

Prayer of Supplication

Supplication is defined as or translated meaning a request or petition.

> "I exhort therefore, that, first of all, supplications, prayers, intercessions, and giving of thanks, be made for all men;" (1 Timothy 2:1).

> "Do not fret *or* have any anxiety about anything, but in every circumstance *and* in everything, by prayer and petition (definite requests), with thanksgiving, continue to make your wants known to God," (Philippians 4:6 Amplified Version).

> "Be careful for nothing; but in every thing by prayer and supplication with thanksgiving let your requests be made known unto God," (Philippians 4:6).

The prayer of supplication is a humble, yet heartfelt and earnest prayer request to the Lord. We should never pray or seek the Lord as a last resort but always as a first priority in every area of our lives and for others. When we pray the prayer of supplication, these are specific requests that are heartfelt before the Lord.

Prayer of Faith

> "And the prayer of faith shall save the sick, and the Lord shall raise him up; and if he have committed sins, they shall be forgiven him," (James 5:15).

"Prayers offered in faith will restore them from sickness *and bring them to health.* The Lord will lift them up *from the floor of despair;* and if the sickness is due to sin, then God will forgive their sins,"
(James 5:15 Voice translation).

The prayer of faith I believe is exemplified in verse 16 as well in the same chapter of James.

"Confess your faults one to another, and pray one for another, that you may be healed. **The effectual fervent prayer of a righteous man avails much**,"
(James 5:16 bold added for emphasis).

"Confess to one another therefore your faults (your slips, your false steps, your offenses, your sins) and pray [also] for one another, that you may be **healed** *and* **restored** [to a spiritual tone of mind and heart]. **The earnest (heartfelt, continued) prayer of a righteous man makes tremendous power available [dynamic in its working]**," (James 5:16 Amplified Version-bold added for emphasis).

I believe when James wrote this epistle or letter, verses 15 and 16 are indicative of the power of the prayer of faith which will bring restoration to the lives of others. These prayers are showing forth tremendous power and dynamic in its working. Now, that is not to say that all of the prayers before mentioned are not powerful or dynamic because they are, however without faith it is impossible to please God, (Hebrews 11:6). Now, in order for the prayer of faith to be effectively prayed, it is imperative that all parties present are in faith and not in doubt. The prayer of supplication does not require others to be present; however the prayer of faith involves more than one person being present. You might ask yourself the question, well then what is the difference between the prayer of faith and the prayer of agreement? The prayer of agreement does not necessarily require supernatural

110

intervention, i.e. praying for a home, or a car, or a promotion on a job, but the prayer of faith does. The prayer of agreement might require favor; however the prayer of faith requires the supernatural power of God to manifest to bring change, healing and restoration.

Prayer of Dedication and Consecration

The Prayer of Dedication and Consecration is shown in the lives of Hannah who was the Prophet Samuel's mother and in our Lord's life prior to His crucifixion.

> [9] So Hannah rose up after they had eaten in Shiloh, and after they had drunk. Now Eli the priest sat upon a seat by a post of the temple of the LORD.
> [10] And she was in bitterness of soul, and prayed unto the LORD, and wept sore.
> [11] And she vowed a vow, and said, O LORD of hosts, if thou wilt indeed look on the affliction of thine handmaid, and remember me, and not forget thine handmaid, but wilt give unto thine handmaid a man child, then I will give him unto the LORD all the days of his life, and there shall no razor come upon his head, (1 Samuel 1:9-11).

Hannah kept her word to the Lord.

> "But Hannah went not up; for she said unto her husband, I will not go up until the child be weaned, and then I will bring him, that he may appear before the LORD, and there abide for ever,"   (1 Samuel 1:22).

> [27] For this child I prayed; and the LORD hath given me my petition which I asked of him:
> [28] Therefore also I have lent him to the LORD; as long as he lives he shall be lent to the LORD. And he worshipped the LORD there,   (1 Samuel 1:27-28).

Hannah did petition before the Lord for a child. He blessed her to conceive. She dedicated and consecrated her baby by taking him to the house of the Lord once he was weaned and was a child. Wow! Her son Samuel was a mighty prophet and judge for Israel. What love Hannah had for God to be willing to give up her first born son! The Lord blessed her though. She went from being barren to giving birth to more sons and daughters.

> "And the LORD visited Hannah, so that she conceived, and bare three sons and two daughters. And the child Samuel grew before the LORD," (1 Samuel 2:21).

The prayer of Dedication and Consecration is a prayer of sacrifice. We read this when our Lord prayed in the Garden of Gethsemane.

> "And he went a little farther, and fell on his face, and prayed, saying, O my Father, if it be possible, let this cup pass from me: nevertheless not as I will, but as thou wilt," (Matthew 26:39).

When praying this prayer, it is a matter of surrendering ones will to the Lord's ultimate will. Children are dedicated to the Lord in church to this day. It is a blessing for babies and children to be dedicated to the Lord. Consecration is a matter of setting apart or purifying. The prayer of Dedication and Consecration is selfless and sacrificial. To say, "Lord, not my will, your will be done," and to be willing to give back to the Lord the very thing desired of Him is powerful.

The Prayer of Thanksgiving

King David was a man who was forever grateful to the Lord. All throughout the Psalms we can read prayers of thanksgiving to the Lord for the great things He has done. I get concerned when I see Christians pray to the Lord, get their prayers answered, and very seldom or hardly say thank you to the Lord.

The Lord loves when we thank Him, worship Him, praise Him. Referencing Philippians 4:6 again, we as Christians are admonished to add thanksgiving to our prayers. We cannot manipulate God, we cannot take God for granted, but we surely can touch the heart of God with our thanksgiving. All throughout the Gospels, we read in scriptures when Jesus healed people they went about rejoicing and thanking the Lord.

Is it possible that we can have our prayers answered but perhaps not in the fullness of what the Lord desires for us because thanksgiving was not included? There were 10 lepers that sought the Lord for healing and out of ten only one came back to say thank you. That one leper was not only healed but he was also made whole.

> ¹⁵ And one of them, when he saw that he was healed, turned back, and with a loud voice glorified God,
> ¹⁶ And fell down on his face at his feet, **giving him thanks**: and he was a Samaritan.
> ¹⁷ And Jesus answering said, Were there not ten cleansed? but where are the nine?
> ¹⁸ There are not found that returned to give glory to God, save this stranger.
> ¹⁹ And he said unto him, Arise, go thy way: thy faith hath made thee whole,
> (Luke 17:15-19 bold added for emphasis).

The Samaritan who glorified God with a loud voice gave him thanks, and even fell down at His feet was not only cleansed from leprosy but made whole in every area of his life.

This is why it is important to allow people who go to church to glorify the Lord with a loud voice and worship Him. After all, He is God and no one knows what a person is going through or dealing with except that person and the Lord. We must give the Lord thanksgiving in advance and again upon the manifestation of the answer. In fact, all Christians need to live a lifestyle of thanksgiving to the Lord. No not being legalistic, but rather maintaining an attitude of gratitude. We should not praise the Lord only for what's deemed as the big blessings and disregard the smaller blessings, we need to be thankful twenty four hours a day, seven days a week.

In fact, let me encourage you now, after you read this, to stop and begin to offer up the prayer of Thanksgiving for all that you are believing God for. Begin to thank Him for all of the prayers that have already been answered and thank Him for His goodness, for being gracious, for His love, for His protection, etc. When we thank the Lord, He takes pleasure in prospering us knowing our boast will be in Him. Remember, our God is a jealous God. Give Him thanks because of who He is. He is worthy to receive all of your thanksgiving.

Spiritual Weapon #6 Forgiveness

Oftentimes in society, it appears that there are times the offender receives more attention for restoration and help, rather than the victim of the situation. This can leave the person who experienced something negative whether tragic or small to feel as though does anyone care about me? It almost seems as though adding insult to injury is to forgive. However this is what the Lord spoke to my heart about forgiveness: "Let my children know that forgiveness is not the absence of accountability but rather it gives me access to avenge them." That right there is great news and brings a sigh of relief. Christianity will almost appear as though we're being a doormat for evil and wicked perpetrators. Here are some scriptures to further emphasize this point.

> [27] But I say unto you which hear, Love your enemies, do good to them which hate you,
> [28] Bless them that curse you, and pray for them which despitefully use you.
> [29] And unto him that smiteth thee on the one cheek offer also the other; and him that taketh away thy cloak forbid not to take thy coat also, (Luke 6:27-29).
> [21] If thine enemy be hungry, give him bread to eat; and if he be thirsty, give him water to drink:
> [22] For thou shalt heap coals of fire upon his head, and the LORD shall reward thee, "(Proverbs 25:21-22).

"Therefore if thine enemy hunger, feed him; if he thirst, give him drink: for in so doing thou shalt heap coals of fire on his head," (Romans 12:20).

[14] For if ye forgive men their trespasses, your heavenly Father will also forgive you:

[15] But if ye forgive not men their trespasses, neither will your Father forgive your trespasses,

(Matthew 6:14-15).

The reason why forgiveness is a mighty spiritual weapon against the adversary is because when you forgive others, you are showing forth the love of Jesus. Now let me bring clarity. The Lord does not mean for you to go through life being abused. NO! There are laws against abuse. Whether physical, sexual, elder abuse, child abuse, etc., all forms of abuse are wrong! This is why we have law enforcement and laws to protect people from evil people doing evil things. If someone broke into your home, or broke into your car, office, etc., you have a right to contact the police and press charges. Remember the Lord is for justice and judgment, (Proverbs 21:3). The aforementioned scriptures, the Lord was talking about the attitude of the heart. Do not live life an eye for an eye, but rather walk in forgiveness towards those who do wrong. Now, when you forgive people for the wrong they've done to you, not only are you forgiven of your trespasses, this is what you can expect from the Lord:

"Dearly beloved, avenge not yourselves, but rather give place unto wrath: for it is written, **Vengeance is mine; I will repay, saith the Lord**,"

(Romans 12:19 bold added for emphasis).

"[It is a fair decision] since it is a righteous thing with God **to repay with distress *and* affliction** those who distress *and* afflict you," (2 Thessalonians 1:6 Amplified Version-bold added for emphasis).

"While at the same time he is preparing judgment and punishment for those who are hurting you,"
(2 Thessalonians 1:6 the Living Bible Translation).

"God is just: He will pay back trouble to those who trouble you."
(2 Thessalonians 1:6 New International Version).

"You prepare a table before me in the presence of my enemies; You anoint my head with oil; My cup runs over," (Psalm 23:5 New King James Version-bold added for emphasis).

When we forgive people of all of their wrong doing, rest assured your angels are keeping a record of everything happening to you and they're reporting back to the Lord. The Lord WILL avenge you of every wrong doing that has happened to you. If you were bullied as a child on the playground, someone stole your lunch in high school, the promotion that was for you was given to someone else because of office politics or favoritism, etc. regardless of the negativity that has happened to you, FORGIVE. Do so now. Go before the Lord and let him know you forgive everyone who has ever wronged you. Name names and situations rest assured He can handle it. Be specific. Let Him know you forgive everyone. Trust He will avenge you of all wrong doing and that He will prepare a table for you in the presence of your enemies. Any bad or negative thing that happened to you is not okay. It was wrong. It was bad. I pray that the Lord heals your memories, your physical body, and your emotions in Jesus name.

Not only will the Lord deal with the perpetrator He will also deal with the evil spirits that influenced the person or people of the wrong they had done. The Lord is protective of His children. No one is getting away with anything. As I always say, love everybody and forgive everybody. In doing so, you will watch the Lord, Abba Father deal with the situations on your behalf. So no personal vendettas, do not be vindictive, and do not allow a root of bitterness to spring up in your life. Keep the fruit of the spirit in operation in your life. When you walk in love and forgiveness, you're heaping coals of fire on your enemies head. Forgiveness is a powerful spiritual weapon.

Spiritual Weapon #7 the Name of Jesus

There was a time when hearing the Saints say the name of Jesus was expected in any church service. Now, people can attend a church service, hear someone pray an opening prayer and not even close out the prayer in Jesus name. There is power in the name of Jesus. Demons know this. They tremble at His name.

> "You believe that there is one God. You do well. Even the demons believe — and tremble!" (James 2:19 New King James Version).

> [9] Wherefore God also hath highly exalted him, and given him a name which is above every name:
> [10] That at the name of Jesus every knee should bow, of things in heaven, and things in earth, and things under the earth;
> [11] And that every tongue should confess that Jesus Christ is Lord, to the glory of God the Father, (Philippians 2:9-11).
> [13] And whatsoever ye shall ask in my name, that will I do, that the Father may be glorified in the Son.
> [14] If ye shall ask any thing in my name, I will do it, (John 14:13-14).
> [17] And these signs shall follow them that believe; **In my name** shall they cast out devils; they shall speak with new tongues;
> [18] They shall take up serpents; and if they drink any deadly thing, it shall not hurt them; they shall lay hands on the sick, and they shall recover,
> (Mark 16:17-18 bold added for emphasis).

Our power and authority in the earth realm to heal the sick, cast out demons, raise the dead, commanding demons to flee, etc. is all done in the all powerful name of Jesus!

> "Neither is there salvation in any other: for there is
> none other name under heaven given among men,
> whereby we must be saved,"   (Acts 4:12).

Salvation is ONLY in the name of Jesus! Prayers are answered ONLY in the name of Jesus! Casting out demons is ONLY in the name of Jesus! Our victory as Christians is ONLY in the all powerful name of Jesus!

Every Christian needs to speak the name of Jesus. Even if every Christian does not receive the Baptism of the Holy Spirit and never speak in other tongues, every Christian still needs to pray and say the name of Jesus!

Spiritual Weapon #8 the Blood of Jesus

> "And they overcame him by the **blood of the Lamb,**
> and by the word of their testimony; and they loved
> not their lives unto the death,"
>   (Revelation 12:11-bold added for emphasis).

The Blood of Jesus provides protection, forgiveness of sins, redemption, restoration, healing, and wholeness. This is why it is imperative for Churches to take time to reverence Communion. It is a reminder of the Lord's great love for us and the horrible events He experienced after He was in the Garden of Gethsemane and prior to His crucifixion.

> [26] And as they were eating, Jesus took bread, and
> blessed it, and brake it, and gave it to the disciples,
> and said, Take, eat; this is my body.

²⁷ And he took the cup, and gave thanks, and gave it to them, saying, Drink ye all of it;
²⁸ For this is my blood of the new testament, which is shed for many for the remission of sins.

(Matthew 26:26-28).

"And almost all things are by the law purged with blood; and without shedding of blood is no remission," (Hebrews 9:22).

"For the life of the flesh is in the blood: and I have given it to you upon the altar to make an atonement for your souls: for it is the blood that maketh an atonement for the soul," (Leviticus 17:11).

Read Exodus chapter 12 in its entirety to understand the Passover and what occurred in Egypt with an animal, a lamb. Our Lord Jesus became the Lamb of God. His death, the ultimate sacrifice for all of mankind, is the reason why as Christians; we eat of His flesh and drink of His blood symbolically by taking Communion. Praise the Lord He rose from the dead! Jesus is alive!

"For the LORD will pass through to smite the Egyptians; and when he seeth the blood upon the lintel, and on the two side posts, the LORD will pass over the door, and will not suffer the destroyer to come in unto your houses to smite you," (Exodus 12:23).

"Then Jesus said unto them, Verily, verily, I say unto you, Except ye eat the flesh of the Son of man, and drink his blood, ye have no life in you," (John 6:53).

"And all that dwell upon the earth shall worship him, whose names are not written in the book of life **of the Lamb slain from the foundation of the world,** (Revelation 13:8 bold added for emphasis).

The plan of salvation through the Lord's shed blood was from the foundation of the world.

The blood of animals was not sufficient for mankind's redemption. We have been purchased back by the Blood of Jesus, that's what redemption is, a purchase.

> "In whom we have **redemption through his blood, the forgiveness of sins,** according to the riches of his grace;" (Ephesians 1:7).

The Lord's body was broken for us and His blood shed for us. This is why there is so much power in the Blood of Jesus! Even as the Jewish people applied the blood of lambs on their doorposts and lentils for protection, we too in our New Covenant can apply the Blood of Jesus to cover our homes, cars, businesses, children, neighborhood, job, etcetera. How is this done you might wonder? You do so by symbolically touching all of these areas with your hands and say "I plead the Blood of Jesus." When you go through your home, you can touch doors, door knobs, door posts, and windows saying out loud I plead the Blood of Jesus. This is symbolic of what happened in the Old Covenant, we can do in the New Covenant because of our Lord Jesus.

Parents or guardians, you can lay hands on your children by touching their foreheads and say out loud, "I plead the Blood of Jesus." It is in His Blood that we have health, life, protection, redemption. We are forgiven of our sins and cleansed from all unrighteousness because of the Blood of Jesus, (1 John 1:9).

The adversary knows how powerful the Blood of Jesus is against him. When we plead the Blood, he is reminded of eternal defeat!

> "Which none of the princes of this world knew: for had they known it, they would not have crucified the Lord of glory," (1 Corinthians 2:8).

The Blood of Jesus causes deliverance. The Blood of Jesus brings sanctification and holiness.

"And such were some of you: but ye are washed, but
ye are sanctified, but ye are justified in the name of
the Lord Jesus, and by the Spirit of our God,"
(1 Corinthians 6:11).

We are not holy, justified, or righteous by the blood of animals,
nor by our own works, but it is only through the Blood of Jesus.
This is the reason why we overcome the devil by the Blood of the
Lamb and the word of our testimony. The Blood of Jesus is against
satan and every demonic spirit hallelujah! Plead the Blood of Jesus,
sing songs about the Blood of Jesus; the Blood will NEVER lose its
power, glory to God!

Spiritual Weapon #9 Love

God is love. Jesus loves you. This is truth not cliché'. The Lord
told us He gives us a new commandment, and that is to love one
another even as He loves us, (John 13:34). Agape love is unconditional. 1 Corinthians chapter 13 referred to as the Love Chapter,
describes in detail what love really is. The love of God is patient. The
love of God is kind. The love of God is not easily provoked. The love
of God is not envious. The love of God is powerful. In fact, the Lord
said it is because of the love that we have towards one another that
the world will know we are His disciples.

"By this shall all men know that you are my disciples,
if you have love one to another,"   (John 13:35).

Based on these scriptures, we can do so many wonderful things for
people; feed the poor, donate money, clothe those in need, and even
become a martyr by having our bodies burned alive. HOWEVER, if
any of these things are not done in love then it's done in vain.

Satan hates love because love represents the Lord. The Lord does
not have love, He is love. And His love has been shed abroad in our
hearts by the Holy Spirit, (Romans 5:5). Therefore we are able to
love our enemies because of the Holy Spirit, (Matthew 5:44).

Love is a powerful weapon against the adversary because love casts out fear.

"There is no fear in love; but perfect love casts out fear: because fear hath torment. He that fears is not made perfect in love,"   (1 John 4:18).

"For God hath not given us the spirit of fear; but of power, **and of love**, and of a sound mind,"
                    (2 Timothy 1:7 bold added for emphasis).

Love casts out all forms of fear. Love casts out the spirit of fear. When we walk in love, we walk in Christ. We represent Christ. We are being obedient to His new commandment, and commandments are not options or suggestions.

Read 1 John 4:7-30 and meditate and memorize these important passages of scripture written by the Apostle John. Love will protect you and also propel you into the deeper realms of God and to even receive the mysteries of God. There were things the Apostle John witnessed that he was not allowed to record or write about such things, (Revelation 10:4).

When we love someone we want to spend time with them. We desire to commune with them and fellowship with them. So it is for our Father in Heaven. He loves us so much, that the Greater One dwells in us (1 John 4:4).

Our love is a spiritual weapon against the adversary because Jesus is love and love is greater than hate. The late great, Dr. Martin Luther King, Jr. exemplified love. His non violence approach to the ills of the South caused laws to be changed and lives to be enhanced and protected.

"Hate cannot drive out hate: only love can do that,"
                    Dr. Martin Luther King, Jr.

When we show people the love of God, we are walking in freedom from fear. We are driving out hatred. We are showing the world Jesus. Love is a powerful weapon! As Christians, let us love the Lord, love one another, love our enemies, and let us not forget to love ourselves. All too often people will love others more than themselves. We are to love people as we love ourselves, not more than or less than, (Mark 12:31).

Faith works by love, (Galatians 5:6). Could it be possible that Christians "shield of faith" is not quenching fiery darts because their love has waxed cold? (Matthew 24:12) We are given a new commandment from the Lord which is to love.

Part Three:

Heavenly Operations against Satan's Rank & File the Demonic Hierarchy

Chapter Seven:

Heavenly Operations

—⁓⁓⁓—

There are a plethora of scriptures from the Old and New Testaments that can be read regarding our spiritual weapons. I only shared a few. The Word of God is vast, filled with so much revelation. The Word of God is alive and powerful. As you continue to study the Word of God and spend time communing with the Holy Spirit, He will continue to lead you and guide you in further truths. These truths can be applied to every area of your life. This book is to help you as a study guide, a handbook, so you can be a doer of the Word and not a hearer only or in this case a reader only, (James 1:22).

We wrestle not against flesh and blood, but against principalities, against powers, against the rulers of the darkness of this world, against spiritual wickedness in high places, (Ephesians 6:12).

To reiterate, I'm not stating there are only nine spiritual weapons in our Heavenly Arsenal. These are the nine the Lord revealed to me. We also have powerful supernatural spiritual backup to use with our spiritual weapons against satan's hierarchy. These are the special operations for all Believers. Some of our powerful backup include; the Chariots of God, Chariots of Fire, the Lord as a hedge of protection as a wall of fire, Cherubim and Flaming Swords of Fire, Seraphim, Warring Angels, Ministering Angels & Ministering Spirits (flame of fire), spirit of adoption, and the spirit of grace and supplication.

> "The chariots of God are twenty thousand, even thou-
> sands of angels: the Lord is among them, as in Sinai,
> in the holy place,"   (Psalm 68:17).

We have a right to ask the Lord to send forth His chariots into neighborhoods and in cities, states, and countries where there's unrest and much destruction. By doing so, we know there are at least TWENTY THOUSAND going forth! That's powerful! The angels and the Lord Himself accompany such chariots.

> "And Elisha prayed, and said, LORD, I pray thee, open
> his eyes, that he may see. And the LORD opened the
> eyes of the young man; and he saw: and, behold, the
> mountain was **full of horses and chariots of fire**
> round about Elisha,"   (2 Kings 6:17).

I even pray for myself, my family members, friends, relatives, and loved ones that the Lord will be a hedge of protection even as a wall of fire around and about us.

> "For I, saith the LORD, will be unto her a wall of fire
> round about, and will be the glory in the midst of
> her,"   (Zechariah 2:5).

The Lord alone is omnipresent. Angels are not, demons are not, and satan is not. Only the Lord is. We can ask the Lord to be a wall of fire round about us, protecting us from all hurt, harm, and danger.

> "So he drove out the man; and he placed at the east of
> the garden of Eden **Cherubims, and a flaming sword**
> **which turned every way**, to keep the way of the tree
> of life,"   (Genesis 3:24 bold added for emphasis).

The Seraphim declare the Lord's holiness and glory in the earth. In the year that king Uzziah died I saw also the LORD sitting upon a throne, high and lifted up, and his train filled the temple.

² Above it stood the seraphims: each one had six wings; with twain he covered his face, and with twain he covered his feet, and with twain he did fly.

³ And one cried unto another, and said, Holy, holy, holy, is the LORD of hosts: the whole earth is full of his glory.

⁴ And the posts of the door moved at the voice of him that cried, and the house was filled with smoke.

⁵ Then said I, Woe is me! for I am undone; because I am a man of unclean lips, and I dwell in the midst of a people of unclean lips: for mine eyes have seen the King, the LORD of hosts.

⁶ Then flew one of the seraphims unto me, having a live coal in his hand, which he had taken with the tongs from off the altar:

⁷ And he laid it upon my mouth, and said, Lo, this hath touched thy lips; and thine iniquity is taken away, and thy sin purged.

⁸ Also I heard the voice of the Lord, saying, Whom shall I send, and who will go for us? Then said I, Here am I; send me   (Isaiah 6:1-8).

When I go somewhere to minister the Word, I ask the Lord to send forth His Seraphim in the service so the glory and holiness of our great God will be a tangible presence. If there's a place where there's strife or contention, ask the Lord to send forth His Seraphim into the situation. The Lord sometimes will allow His people to go into a spiritual atmosphere of chaos so the presence of the Lord can bring peace.

Warring angels, ministering angels, and ministering spirits can go forth and do battle on our behalf in the heavenlies, in the earth, in the sea, under the earth. The warring angels have their swords. They use their swords against satan and his demonic hierarchy. Remember, satan is the god of this world and he is the prince of the power of the air (2 Corinthians 4:4, Ephesians 2:2). You can send forth the warring angels to fight imps, demons, and war against and bind up satan which is for a season. Remember when Jesus was tempted of the devil in the wilderness the Word of God teaches us he left Him for a season.

> "Are they not all ministering spirits, sent forth to minister for them who shall be heirs of salvation?"
> (Hebrews 1:14).

> "Therefore, angels are only servants—spirits sent to care for people who will inherit salvation,"
> (Hebrews 1:14 New Living Translation).

> "The heavenly messengers are only spirits and servants, sent out to minister to those who will certainly inherit salvation,"
> (Hebrews 1:14b the Voice Translation).

> "Who makes his angels spirits; his ministers a flaming fire:" (Psalm 104:4).

> "The angels are his messengers—his servants of fire!" (Psalm 104:4 the Living Bible).

> "And of the angels he says, Who makes his angels spirits, and his ministers a flame of fire," (Hebrews 1:7).

You can send forth the ministering angels who are ministering spirits of fire. Send them to your children's schools, in their classrooms, to unsaved family members, and loved ones to minister to them and serve them. Pray for these individuals to become heirs of salvation and for their protection.

Spirit of adoption helps people to be delivered from strongholds such as substance abuse.

Romans 8:15 Amplified Version-" For [the Spirit which] you have now received [is] not a spirit of slavery to put you once more in bondage to fear, but you have received the Spirit of adoption [the Spirit producing sonship] in [the bliss of] which we cry, Abba (Father)! Father!"

Romans 8:15-17 Message Translation- "This resurrection life you received from God is not a timid, grave-tending life. It's adventurously expectant, greeting God with a childlike "What's next, Papa?" God's Spirit touches our spirits and confirms who we really are. We know who he is, and we know who we are: Father and children. And we know we are going to get what's coming to us—an unbelievable inheritance! We go through exactly what Christ goes through. If we go through the hard times with him, then we're certainly going to go through the good times with him!"

Romans 8:15 King James Version- "For you have not received the spirit of bondage again to fear; but you have received the Spirit of adoption, whereby we cry, Abba, Father."

In these scriptures, it is clear that there is a spirit of bondage and the Spirit of adoption. Whenever you see someone living in bondage to sin or have a stronghold in his or her life, you can intercede and pray for their deliverance from bondage. The Spirit of adoption who is the Holy Spirit will set them free.

The Spirit of grace and supplications as described in Zechariah is for people to see the magnitude of what the Lord has done for us. "And I will pour upon the house of David, and upon the inhabitants of Jerusalem, the spirit of grace and of supplications: and they shall look upon me whom they have pierced, and they shall mourn for him, as one mourns for his only son, and shall be in bitterness for him, as one that is in bitterness for his firstborn," Zechariah 12:10 King James Version.

> "And I will pour out upon the house of David and upon the inhabitants of Jerusalem the Spirit of grace *or* unmerited favor and supplication. And they shall look [earnestly] upon Me Whom they have pierced, and they shall mourn for Him as one mourns for his only son, and shall be in bitterness for Him as one who is in bitterness for his firstborn,"
>
> Zechariah 12:10 Amplified Version.

"Next I'll deal with the family of David and those
who live in Jerusalem. I'll pour a spirit of grace and
prayer over them. They'll then be able to recognize
me as the One they so grievously wounded—that
piercing spear-thrust! And they'll weep—oh, how
they'll weep! Deep mourning as of a parent grieving
the loss of the firstborn child,"
                Zechariah 12:10 Message Translation.

The Spirit of Grace and supplications or prayer are the manifestations of the Holy Spirit. When we ask the Holy Spirit to reveal
Himself to unsaved family members, His grace covers them and they
are able to come to a place of conviction and convincing as then they
are able to see Lord as the One brutally beaten for their sins. The Lord
did not die a simple death for all of mankind, He was beaten beyond
recognition, spat upon, and his beard pulled off His face.
Isaiah 52:14 New Living Translation

"But many were amazed when they saw him. His face
was so disfigured he seemed hardly human, and from
his appearance, one would scarcely know he was a
man."   Isaiah 50:6 New Living Translation

"I offered my back to those who beat me and my
cheeks to those who pulled out my beard. I did not
hide my face from mockery and spitting."

When the Lord endured such brutality for all of mankind's
redemption, satan and his demons were convinced they were getting rid of the Lord once and for all. For the Bible teaches us that if
they only knew, they would have never crucified the Lord.

"No, the wisdom we speak of is the mystery of God—
his plan that was previously hidden, even though he
made it for our ultimate glory before the world began.
But the rulers of this world have not understood it; if

they had, they would not have crucified our glorious Lord," 1 Corinthians 2:7-8 New Living Translation.

This is the life of the Believer in a nutshell as it were. The Word of God and the things of God are a part of the mysteries of God. This is not based in logic but rather established in faith that can only be perceived and revealed by the Holy Spirit. This is why spiritual warfare is fought and won only in the realm of the Spirit and not in carnality or in the flesh.

Chapter Eight:

Glorious Church

> [27] *He has given Himself* so that He can present the church as His radiant bride, unstained, unwrinkled, and unblemished—*completely free from all impurity*—holy and innocent before Him. (Hebrews 5:27 the Voice Translation)

In essence, Department of Defense here in the United States of America is a highly classified organization for the purpose of protecting human life. Examples of some Special Ops/Special Forces are Air Force Special Tactics, Army Green Berets, Marine Reconnaissance, and Navy Seals. This requires a more highly trained and rigorous assessment for those who desire a more specialized service in the military.

Our ally Israel, has the Iron Dome which is a missile defense system which is designed to intercept AND destroy short range rockets and artillery shells. The Lord spoke to my heart last year and He said "What the Iron Dome is in the natural is what the Shield of Faith is in the spiritual." WOW! I was so excited the Lord would share that with me! That is a visual of our spiritual military weaponry designed by the Lord to assist us to live victorious lives as His sons and daughters. Our Shield of Faith is designed to quench EVERY fiery dart from the wicked. Glory to God!

1 Corinthians 12:4-11King James Version (KJV)

[4] Now there are diversities of gifts, but the same Spirit.
[5] And there are differences of administrations, but the same Lord.

[6] And there are diversities of operations, but it is the same God which worketh all in all.

[7] But the manifestation of the Spirit is given to every man to profit withal.
[8] For to one is given by the Spirit the word of wisdom; to another the word of knowledge by the same Spirit;
[9] To another faith by the same Spirit; to another the gifts of healing by the same Spirit;
[10] To another the working of miracles; to another prophecy; to another discerning of spirits; to another divers kinds of tongues; to another the interpretation of tongues:
[11] But all these worketh that one and the selfsame Spirit, dividing to every man severally as he will.

The King James version teaches diversities of operations, even the Military have Special Operations. It is so imperative for the Gifts of the Spirit to be in operation in the lives of Believers not just in the local church, but wherever and whenever the Holy Spirit wills. The Holy Spirit can very easily instruct someone to give a Word of Knowledge or a Word of Wisdom to someone at the grocery store, manifest with the gift of healing at a bank, discerning of spirits at a concert, etc. These are special operations and every Christian does not operate in these gifts. Again, it is as the Holy Spirit wills.

These "Special Operations" are so imperative. In these last days, deception will run rampant. There are Christians who go to psychics and people who believe there are "good witches" and "bad witches" based on black magic and white magic. These gifts of the Spirit will expose what satan is plotting and planning because the Holy Spirit is Truth and He cannot lie. It is impossible for God to lie.

This is why Christians need to understand there are "presents than can carry an evil presence," as the Lord instructed me. This is evident in the Book of Acts.

> [19] Many of them also which used curious arts brought their books together, and burned them before all men: and they counted the price of them, and found it fifty thousand pieces of silver.
> [20] So mightily grew the word of God and prevailed.

When traveling to other countries, all "souvenirs" are not to be taken out their country of origin. There are some items that are actually "prayed" over giving demonic spirits access. This is why as Christians we cannot listen to all genres of music and Ouija boards are not mere games. Those boards are demonic. Horoscopes, psychics and mediums are all of the devil. In the Old Testament, people who practiced such came under the judgment of God and were put to death. In the New Testament, because of the Blood of Jesus, salvation and redemption are available for people to come out of darkness and be translated into the Lord's marvelous light.

The Apostle Paul gives us a military command in the Book of Ephesians to stand. In the military, when given the command "Attention!" the soldiers immediately stand at attention with a specific posture. Even "parade rest," or "at ease" are still commands, yet the posture and stance changes. Ephesians 6:11-17, the word STAND is mentioned three times. Evidently the Holy Spirit through the Apostle Paul is emphasizing the importance of such. Standing for long periods of time can cause fatigue. That is why when the "Operations" of the Holy Spirit such as prophecy manifest, edification, exhortation, and comfort takes place. No Christian is exempt from needing to be edified, built up, encouraged or comforted.

All Christians encounter spiritual warfare, and all Christians are drafted in the army of the Lord. Everyone who claims the Lord is not necessarily known by the Lord. There are those in church who have experienced "friendly fire." Friendly fire is a military term. This is fire that should be directed towards the enemy but instead this fire that comes from one's own side including an ally and can cause accidental injury or even death to one's own forces. An example of this is church hurt. There are too many wounded Christian warriors from friendly fire and church hurt. There is the Wounded Warriors Project, a non-profit organization to help wounded veterans. There are also wounded warriors in the Body of Christ. We need to pray for our Veterans and active duty military men and women. We need to pray for those who have experienced spiritual friendly fire and church hurt to be healed.

Putting on the WHOLE armor of God, and not only knowing that we have spiritual weapons, but also how to use our spiritual weapons will ensure the victory in every area of our lives. Our Lord Christ Jesus has already whipped and defeated satan and all of his diabolical demonic entities. This is why if Christians see shadows in their home, they must take an inventory of what's attracting such activity. We have been given power and authority by our Lord Jesus Christ. As long as we stay connected to Him as greater than any Commander in Chief, Emperor, or General, we have the victory. After all, the Lord is the only King who will never be dethroned! The King of Glory is coming back for His glorious Church. Thank you King Jesus for giving us the victory over the adversary satan and his kingdom. Jesus is Lord of all!

Bibliography

http://www.Oxforddictionaries.com
http://www.BibleGateway.com
http://www.military.com
http://www.soldier.net
http://www.Airforce.com
http://www.Goarmy.com
http://www.Marines.com
http://www.Navy.com
http://www.uscg.mil
http://www.nsa.gov
http://www.thefreedictionary.com
http://www.dailymail.co.uk/news/article-1382859/Osama-bin-Laden-dead-Photo-Obama-watching-Al-Qaeda-leader-die-live-TV.html.
http://www.Wikipedia.com
http://www.huffingtonpost.com
http://www.drmartinlutherkingjr.com/mlkquotes.htm

Prayer of Salvation

Eternal life is only in Christ Jesus. Every person born is born a sinner. Salvation is only in Christ Jesus. In order to receive eternal life, a person must be born again.

Pray this prayer aloud to accept Jesus as your Lord and Savior:

Lord Jesus, I am a sinner. I believe that you died for my sins and that God raised you from the dead. I ask you to come into my heart. I repent of all of my sins. I ask you to become my Lord and Savior. Thank you Lord Jesus for forgiving me of all of my sins, and for giving me a new life in you. In Jesus name I pray, amen.

If you prayed this prayer, all of Heaven is rejoicing over you right now! Welcome to the family of God in Christ Jesus!

To contact Prophetess Leticia Lewis, email her at majesticministriesintl@gmail.com

CPSIA information can be obtained
at www.ICGtesting.com
Printed in the USA
FSHW021834290819
61503FS